1. WHAT IS A PERSONAL COMPUTER?

WHAT MAKES IT A "PERSONAL" COMPUTER?

The term "personal computer" (and the similar term "home computer") is used for computers that are small in size and price (and capability), and that require no special electrical or air-conditioning considerations. The term became popular when several models of computers were available for under $1000 in the late '70s, but now is applied to computers with a base price as high as three to five thousand dollars. To the individual, the term probably implies a computer that is affordable, but with the wide range of prices, the computer for your own personal use ultimately will depend on your budget.

WHAT IS A COMPUTER?

Examine a handheld calculator. It has a keypad for entering numbers (called *data*) and operations, such as $5+10$, $1054-876$, 6×25, and so forth. If you have calculations that require the use of the same number over and over, you can purchase a calculator with a memory location that allows you to save a value and use it later. The calculator has a one-line display at the top that shows you the last calculation or number entered. This is fine for a few calculations, but suppose you have many numbers and calculations. Then you need some method to keep track of where you are. So, in order to facilitate the procedure, let's suppose you have developed a connecting cable (called an *interface*) that allows the calculator display to be attached to a television screen. Now you can use the television screen as the display and have the calculator send the numbers and results to it instead of to the calculator display. In this way, you can look at several lines at the same time as they appear one after another on the television screen (the way the film credits roll at the beginning or the end of a movie). The new lines appear at the bottom of the screen and the lines already present move up the screen. The earlier results may have rolled off at the top of the screen (as with movie credits), but you can see the last few; they will help you keep track of what you've done.

Many times after using a calculator, you may wonder if you keyed in all the numbers and operations correctly. In case of doubt, you go through the calculations again to check yourself. To avoid having to do that, you can trade your handheld calculator for a desktop printing calculator that has, in addition to the display, a built-in paper printing device (known as a *printer*) on which the calculator prints numbers, operations, and results. Then you simply can check the paper listing to see if you did everything correctly. With it, you can send results to the display if you just want to look at them, or to the printer if you want to save them on paper (or both).

Suppose, after you have done this, a friend comes by and shows you a list of calculations from his or her printing calculator (maybe a solution to a problem you've been working on). The paper listing is very helpful, but you decide you want to do the same calculations again, with a few changes here and there. Even though your changes require only a few keystrokes on the calculator keypad, you nevertheless have to key in everything else to arrive at the result you want. To make your job easier, you decide to develop a second connecting cable that will allow the calculator keypad and display to be attached to a tape recorder, just as you would connect a radio to the recorder. Now, just as if you were recording a song from the radio, you can press the record switch on the recorder at any time and have it record your keystrokes or the results appearing on the display, or both, onto a magnetic tape cassette. You can have your friend do that from now on, also. Then the next time, he or she can bring you a paper listing of calculations and also a tape cassette containing the keystrokes. You can rewind the tape and press the play switch to have the tape recorder send the keystrokes to your calculator (just as you would replay the song you recorded). You can do the same exact calculations, or you can stop it now then and key in your changes before continuing. Of course, if the tape recorder is replaying the keystrokes your friend used, then it cannot also record your new keystrokes. So you connect a second tape recorder to allow you to replay old keystrokes and also save your new ones and/or the new results. Figure 1.1 illustrates this device.

This rather odd looking contraption is very similar in concept to a computer. A computer consists of a part that does calculations similar to a calculator (known as a *central processing unit* or *CPU*). It allows the user to key in numbers and operations (known as *input*); the computer performs (or executes) the operations and gives the user the results (known as *output*). A computer, however, allows the use of words and characters as well as numbers and operations. So instead of a keypad, a computer has a *keyboard* similar to that on a typewriter. A computer also has a *memory*, but in addition to storing numbers as a calculator does, it also is used for storing operations, words and characters. A computer has a part that allows the user to print the input and output (known as a *printer*) and parts that allow the user to record (or *store*) input and output and reuse it (known as *storage devices*). These are the main parts of a computer—the

HOW TO BUY A PERSONAL COMPUTER

by Carlton Shrum

AN ALFRED HANDY GUIDE

Computer Series Editor:
George Ledin Jr.

ALFRED PUBLISHING CO., INC.
SHERMAN OAKS, CA 91403

Trademark Acknowledgments

The italicized names are registered trademarks of the following companies:

APPLE, WORD PAINTER, APPLE POST Apple Computer Inc.
ATARI Atari, Inc.
AUTOSCRIBE, BOOKKEEPER, MICROSOURCE, TIMEKEEPER The Phoenix Group, Inc.
BASIC Trustees of Dartmouth College
BASIC-80, COBOL-80, MBASIC Microsoft Consumer Products, Inc.
CBASIC2 Compiler Systems, Inc.
CBM, PET, WORDPRO Commodore Business Machines, Inc.
CDOS, CROMIX Cromemco, Inc.
CIS COBOL Micro Focus, Inc.
CP/A, OSS BASIC Optimized Systems Software
CP/M, CP/NET, MP/M Digital Research, Inc.
DATASTAR, WORDSTAR, MAIL-MERGE Micropro International, Inc.
DB MASTER, MICROMEMO, PRICE SHEET Stoneware Microcomputer Products, Inc.
DISCUS Morrow Designs, Inc.
DISKOS Priam, Inc.
EASYWRITER Cap'n Software, Inc.
FLEX, UNI-FLEX Technical Systems Consultants, Inc.
HDOS Heath Data Systems, Inc.
IBM International Business Machines
IMAGINATION MACHINE APF
I/OS Infosoft Systems, Inc.
JRT PASCAL JRT Systems, Inc.
MAGIC WAND Small Business Applications, Inc.
MDOS Monolithic Systems, Inc.
MICROSTAT Ecosoft, Inc.
MMS FORTH Miller Microcomputer Services, Inc.
MULTIBUS Intel Corporation
MULTIVISION, REGENT Applied Digital Data Systems, Inc.
MUSE SOFTWARE, SUPER-TEXT Muse Software
NEWDOS/80 Apparat, Inc.
NORTHSTAR, NORTHWORD, HORIZON, ADVANTAGE North Star Computers
OASIS Phase One, Inc.
ODOS Omnibyte Corporation
OSBORNE 1 Osborne Computer Corporation
PASCAL/M Sorcim
PASCAL/Z Itaca Intersystems, Inc.
PASCAL/MT M.T. Microsystems, Inc.
POLYFORTH FORTH, Inc.
RADIO SHACK, TRS-80, SCRIPSIT Tandy Corporation
REPORT WRITER Carolina Business Computers
SBASIC Topaz Programming
SDOS Software Dynamics
SL5 The Stackworks
SORCERER, ROM PAC, MICROBIZ Exidy Systems
SPINWRITER NEC Information Systems, Inc.
TIMAKER P. Roizen
THE SOURCE Source Telecomputing Corporation
UCSD PASCAL Regents of the University of California
VISICALC Personal Software, Inc.
XEROX Xerox Corporation
Z80, Z80A Zilog Corporation

Cover Design: Paula Bingham Goldstein
Revised November 1983

Alfred Publishing Co., Inc.
15335 Morrison Street
Sherman Oaks, California 91403

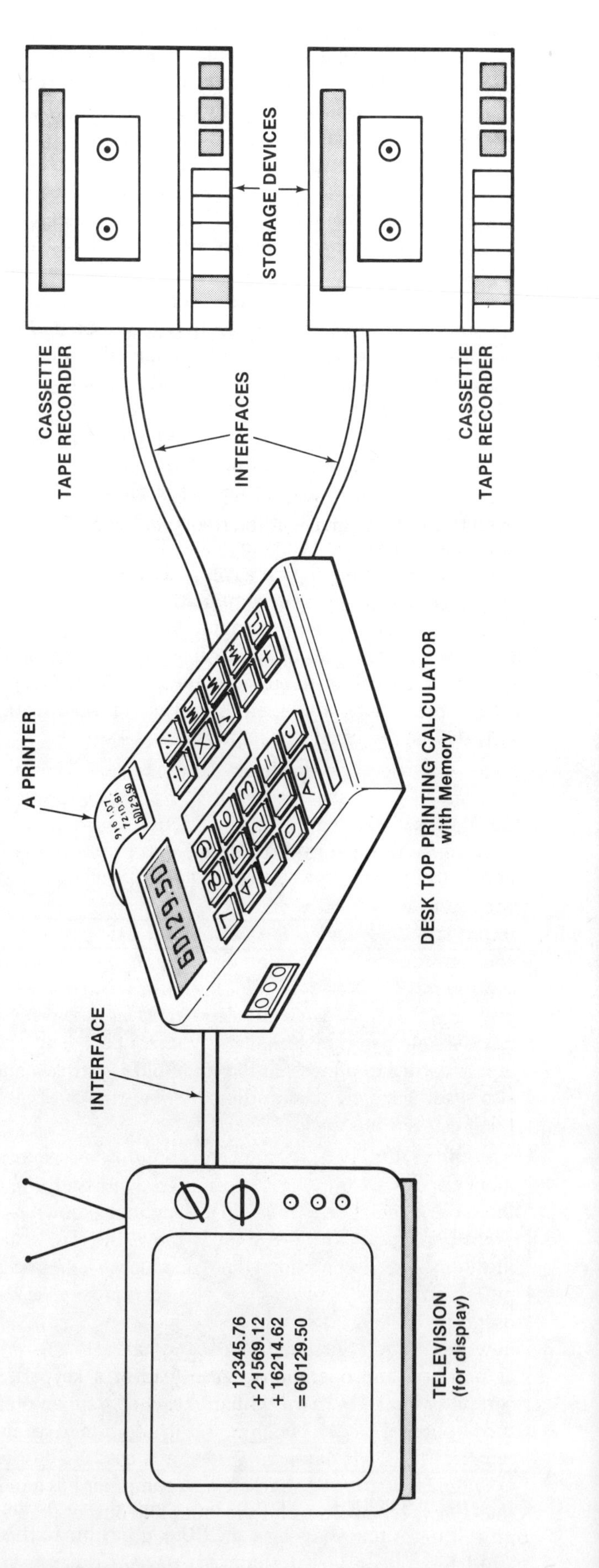

FIGURE 1.1 The components of a simple computer.

central processing unit, the memory, the display, the keyboard, the printer, and the storage devices.

Contrary to what some people believe, a computer has no intelligence. It cannot think or create, but is only a machine. It must be told, step by step, what it is to do, and the range of what it can do is rather limited. It can add, subtract, multiply, divide, make comparisons, manipulate numbers and characters, control other devices that store and retrieve information, and read data and write results. It can do these operations very, very fast. And when the computer is in operation, we have a device that appears very intelligent and very "human." But, again, EVERYTHING has to be told to it—if it works, it was told correctly and if it doesn't work, it was told incorrectly. It is totally dependent on its human operator.

This machine is composed of two parts—*hardware* and *software*. Hardware is the actual physical equipment, anything you can touch and see, such as a cabinet, a connecting cable, a printer, or a storage device. Software is the part that is intangible—it consists of the operations or commands that a computer executes. These work together to give a combination of speed and accuracy that can be used in a large number of applications. Several examples of hardware and software and how they work will be discussed in the next two sections. Actual applications and their hardware and software needs will be discussed in Chapters 3 and 4.

HARDWARE

CPU

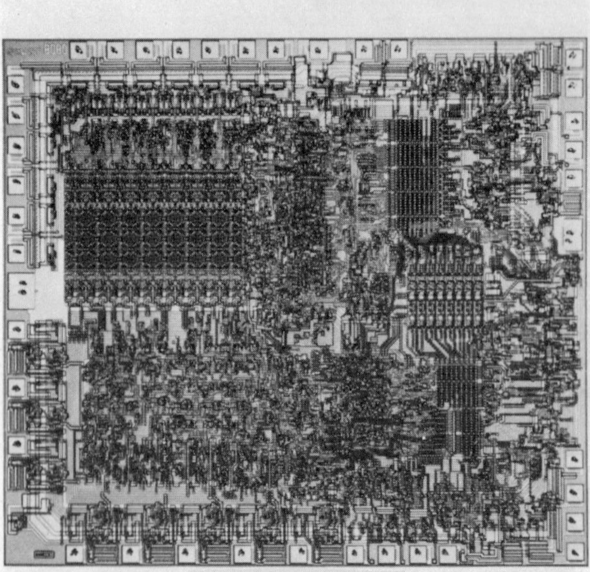

Actual size—13.7mm

FIGURE 1.2 This is a picture of a central processing unit (CPU). A few years ago, a CPU comparible to this would have been larger than this page. Courtesy of Intel Corporation.

The most important piece of hardware is the *CPU*—the central processing unit. The CPU is the "brain" of the computer, the part that does the calculating, the comparing, the manipulating, and the controlling of all of the other units. This is the part that receives orders or commands (called *instructions*) from a user. For instance, "add two numbers, X & Y," "print the result," "determine if X is greater than Y," "save the value of Y," and so forth are instructions. It is extremely fast in its execution of these instructions, often on the order of millions or billions of instructions per second. Improved CPU technology has been one of the major reasons for the lower costs and smaller sizes of computers. Some CPU's are actually no larger than a pencil eraser!

There are two basic types of CPU's used in personal computers: *8-bit* and *16-bit*. Without going into technical detail, the 16-bit CPU is somewhat faster and, more importantly, able to handle more memory than the 8-bit. These two types of CPU's are incompatible, that is, programs that run on one cannot run on the other. This creates a dilemma: Buy a machine that has an 8-bit CPU, since 8-bit personal computers have been around longer and have more programs written for them? Or go with the future *and* 16-bit technology? One solution: Buy a machine that includes both.

MEMORY

Since the CPU can execute instructions at very high speeds, it would be a waste of its ability if it were used as the calculator discussed earlier, with the user entering an instruction, the computer executing it, the user entering another instruction, and so forth. However, using *memory*, the user can enter a large number of instructions that are stored in memory and then the CPU can execute them all at one time.

Memory consists of electronic or magnetic cells, each of which contains information. Computer memory is similar in concept to human memory cells except that it is easily erased. (In fact, most memory found in computers is erased automatically when the power is turned off.) It is directly connected to the CPU and is the location where the instructions and data are placed for access by the CPU (as well as the results from the execution of the instructions). Any of the memory may be accessed very quickly and it may be accessed in any order, therefore, it generally is referred to as *Random Access Memory*, or *RAM*.

One memory cell is called a *bit*, for ***bi**nary digi**t***. It may contain two possible values: 0 or 1 (thus the term "binary"), reflecting a high or low electrical charge or a positive or negative magnetic charge (like turning a light switch on or off). The cells, or bits, usually are linked together in groups of eight known as *bytes*. Coding systems have been formalized to allow the representation of a character within the computer by a certain combination of 0s and 1s within a byte. Thus, on most computers, one byte of memory represents one character, and the total number of bytes represents the total number of characters that can be stored at any one time. The 0s and 1s also may be combined to form numeric values. The decimal (base 10) numbers with which we are familiar may be coded inside a computer with binary (base 2) numbers. For example, 27, which refers to 2 tens and 7 ones, is equivalent to 11011, which refers to 1 sixteen, 1 eight, 0 fours, 1 two, and 1 one. The number of bytes usually is specified with "K" following (for example, 16K bytes). The K refers to kilo and, though the word "kilo" means 1000, the K, in this case, is exactly equivalent to 1024. Thus 16K bytes means there are 16,384 bytes or 131,072 bits. When you reach 1000K, it is referred to as 1M or 1 mega (million).

There is another type of memory known as *Read Only Memory*, or *ROM*. As the name implies, it cannot be written into (and therefore cannot be altered), but can only be read from. You cannot use it for storing instructions or data. It contains instructions and/or data placed there by the manufacturer in order to perform specific tasks. Other than in the inability to alter its contents, it is similar to RAM in both its structure and its use by the CPU.

The combinations of CPU and memory make up the computer, proper, with all other pieces of hardware known as peripherals. All personal computers contain a CPU and memory, but the type and number of peripherals differ greatly.

MAGNETIC TAPE UNITS—CASSETTES

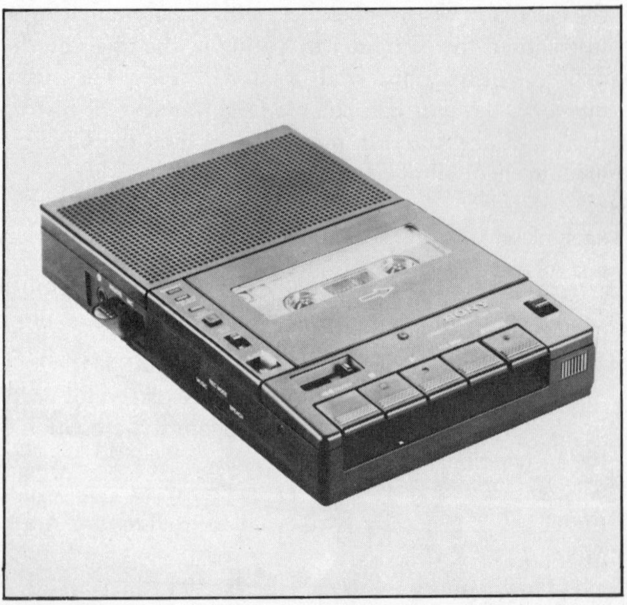

FIGURE 1.3 An ordinary cassette tape recorder often is used as a storage device for a personal computer. Courtesy of Sony Corporation of America.

Memory holds the instructions and data that currently are being used by the CPU. It is capable of storing a limited amount of information, but probably not all of the programs you will ever want to run. Thus, it is usually necessary to extract programs after they are run, and insert new ones. If you had to accomplish this by hand it would be slow and tedious. As a result, *storage devices* were developed. They will store programs not currently being used and will quickly insert or retrieve information from memory. And unlike memory, they will store information even when the power is turned off.

Magnetic tape units often are used as storage devices on personal computers. They range from something as simple as an everyday 1-7/8 inches per second (ips) cassette tape recorder (such as the one connected to the calculator earlier in our discussion) to a professional and expensive high speed (120 ips) reel-to-reel tape unit (known as a tape "drive"), but the principle of operation is the same. For most personal computers, only ordinary cassette units are used, thus no further discussion of tape "drives" will be included.

The speed at which information is transferred between a computer and a cassette unit is measured in bits per second known as *baud rate*). Because of transmission signals which the CPU requires, there is one "start of information transfer" bit and one or two "stop of information transfer" bits associated with each byte (8 bits) of information which is stored. Thus, the number of bytes (or characters) able to be transferred per second is equivalent to the baud rate divided by 10. This speed usually is not dependent on the cassette unit (since all standard cassette units operate at 1-7/8 ips) but is dependent on the computer. Different computers often store different amounts of information per inch of tape. The more information a computer stores per inch of tape, the more information it can transfer each second, and, therefore, the higher the baud rate. Also, higher baud rates, and thus more information stored per inch of tape, mean higher storage capacity per tape. Common baud rates range from 300 to 1500 baud. Some computers offer two baud rates to give the flexibility of one higher speed for normal transfers and one slower speed for compatibility with other computers.

A few personal computers offer cassettes (or cartridges) and cassette (cartridge) units that are more sophisticated than standard audio cassettes and offer higher speed and higher reliability. Baud rates of these units may range as high as 5200 baud. Other high speed cassette-like units may be purchased from independent suppliers (for example, the Exatron Stringy Floppy, the MECA BETA-80, and the JPC TC-8).

DISK UNITS

When you connected the tape recorder to the calculator at the beginning of this chapter, it was noted that after recording information on a tape, the tape had to be rewound before you could reuse that information. Then, when you wanted to intermix the reusing of information and the recording of new information, you needed two tape recorders. Also, if you were at the beginning of a tape and needed information in the middle, you had to take time to fast forward to the desired location. There is a much faster and more convenient storage device, the *disk unit*, which does not have these problems.

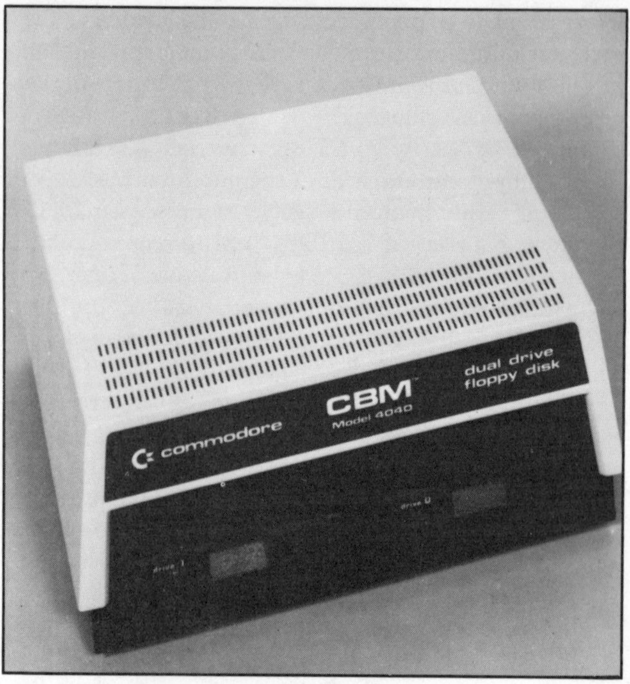

FIGURE 1.4 A disk is a high speed storage device for computers. Courtesy of Commodore Business Machines.

A disk unit (usually referred to simply as a disk) consists of one or more record-like magnetic platters on which to store information, each handled by one read/write head, and a disk drive to turn the platters. A read/write head is a small electromagnetic used for reading, writing (or recording), and erasing information on the surface of a magnetic platter. It sits either just above, or just on, the surface of the platter. The platter is constantly spinning at a very high rate and the head moves in and out, thereby reaching all points on the surface of the platter. In this manner, the disk can be used to read information from one section of the platter and then to write information to another section. This allows the user to intermix old information and record new information as was discussed earlier. Often these platters are interchangeable (similar to changing a record), thus allowing the purchase of one fairly expensive disk unit but many relatively inexpensive platters (known as *packs*, *cartridges*, or *diskettes*, depending on the type of disk unit). Unlike memory, information stored on a disk unit is retained when the power is shut off, as it is with magnetic recording tape.

There are basically two types of disks—hard disks and floppy disks. Hard disks (which are literally hard or stiff) usually are more reliable, will hold much more information (anywhere from 2M bytes to 100M bytes), and are much more expensive. The one or more platters used in a hard disk unit is known as a disk pack or a disk cartridge, depending on the design. The read/write head in a hard disk unit sits just above the platter surface and therefore causes no abrasion of the disk surface.

Floppy disks (which are literally floppy or flexible) usually wear out more quickly (since the head sits on the disk surface), hold from 150K to 1.2M bytes, and are much less expensive. Floppy disk units contain only one interchangeable platter, known as a diskette. Because of their lower cost, floppys are the most popular personal computer storage devices and three basic types have been developed: *a micro-floppy* (3" or 3 1/4" in diameter), a *mini-floppy* (5 1/4" in diameter), and a standard floppy (8" in diameter). Within each size, some disks and disk units use both sides of the disk, therefore doubling the available space overa a single-sided unit. Also, some units store more information in a given amount of area of a platter, providing double or even quadruple the storage of other units. These technological differences between the various disk units account for a large range of storage capacities. Thus, when looking at disk units, it is importnat to note the amount of storage and not only the size of the disk.The chart below compares the storage capacity of different types of disks.

- MICRO-FLOPPY
  Single-sided, 286K (about 114 pages)
  Double-sided, 572K (about 228 pages)
- MINI-FLOPPY
  Single-density, single-sided, about 150K (60 pages)
  Double-density, single-sided or single-density, double-sided, 300K (120 pages)
  Quad-density, single-sided or double-density, double-sided, 600K (240 pages)
- STANDARD FLOPPY
  Single-density, single-sided, 300K (120 pages)
  Double-density, single-sided, 1.2M (480 pages)
- HARD DISKS
  From 2.5M to 100M (1,000 to 40,000 pages!)

The relationship of speed between a tape unit and a disk unit can be compared to that between finding a song on a record and on a cassette. One can find the desired groove (or track) on a record (and, similarly, the desired location on a disk) long before someone else has rewound or fast-forwarded a tape to the desired location. In addition, a disk unit records or retrieves information much faster than a tape unit, with speeds equivalent to a baud rate in the hundreds of thousands or even millions.

DISPLAYS AND KEYBOARDS

As with the unusual calculator discussed at the beginning of this chapter, a *display* device is needed in order to see the transactions occurring between the computer and the user. A few pocket computers have single line displays similar to those on calculators, but the vast majority of personal computers use multi-line displays. The display may actually be a television or it may be a video monitor especially built for use with a computer. As with a television, the display may be black and white or color, depending on what type the computer is able to use. Connected in some way to the display is a typewriter-like *keyboard* for use in typing in instructions and responses to the computer. Some personal computers have an integrated keyboard and display; some include

FIGURE 1.5 A display for a personal computer may be a television set which you already own. Courtesy of Sony Corporation of America.

only the keyboard, and the user must supply the video display; and some include neither, and the user must supply both.

PRINTERS

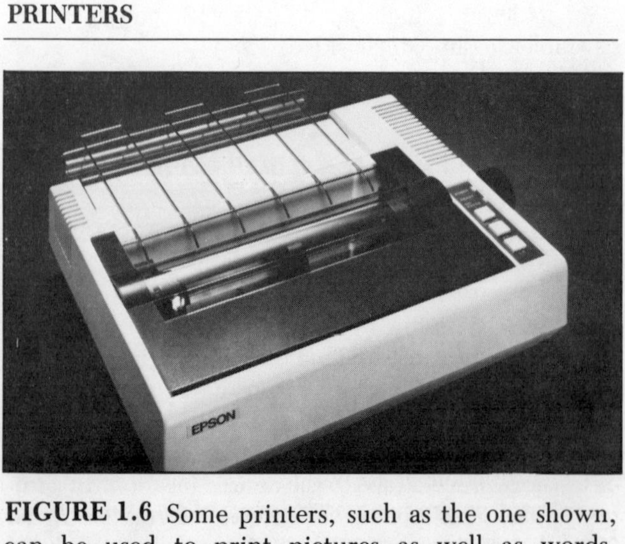

FIGURE 1.6 Some printers, such as the one shown, can be used to print pictures as well as words. Courtesy of Espon America, Inc.

Some applications using computers can be accomplished adequately with only a video display to view the results. However, for most applications, a hard-copy device, or *printer*, is necessary. Some printers are built into the computer as with desk top calculators, but most are externally connected. Some have only upper case letters; others have both upper and lower case. Some have 80-column pages and use standard 8-1/2- x 11-inch paper, while others allow up to 132 columns and may use 14- x 11-inch paper. Some use single paper sheets, some roll paper, and some fanfold perforated paper. Some give typewriter quality printout (often an actual typewriter may be used), and others give lesser quality printout. Some can print graphics (pictures and designs), and some even print in color.

OTHER HARDWARE

There are many other types of hardware, but most are for specialized applications. A few of these will be discussed under the section "What Features Are Important to You?" in Chapter 3.

SOFTWARE

```
100 PRINT "WHAT IS THE NAME OF THE DEMOCRATIC CANDIDATE";
110 INPUT D$
120 PRINT "WHAT IS THE NAME OF THE REPUBLICAN CANDIDATE";
130 INPUT R$
140 LET D=R=T=V=0
150 PRINT
160 PRINT "WHAT IS THE NEXT VOTE-REPORT (D OR R)";
170 INPUT V$
180 IF V$="D" THEN 210
190 IF V$="R" THEN 270
200 GOTO 160
210 LET V=V+1
220 PRINT "HOW MANY ADDITIONAL VOTES FOR ";D$;
230 INPUT X
240 LET D=D+X
250 LET T=T+X
260 GOTO 320
270 LET V=V+1
280 PRINT "HOW MANY ADDITIONAL VOTES FOR ";R$;
290 INPUT X
300 LET R=R+X
310 LET T=T+X
320 PRINT
330 PRINT "NUMBER OF VOTE REPORTS:";V
340 PRINT D$;" (D)",D;"VOTES",100*D/T;"%"
350 PRINT R$;" (R)",R;"VOTES",100*R/T;"%"
360 GOTO 150
370 END
```

FIGURE 1.7 This is a listing of instructions for a computer written in BASIC, the most popular programming language for personal computers.

In order to have a computer accomplish a task (for instance, input 100 numbers, store them, add them, find the average, and output the numbers, their sum, and the average), a sequence of instructions must be given to it, having it to do one step at a time. This sequence of related instructions is known as a *program*. There are two types of programs—system programs and user programs. System programs are those that the CPU executes to manipulate memory, control the various peripherals, and interact with the user. User programs are those that are used to accomplish a particular application, such as the 100 numbers task mentioned above.

THE OPERATING SYSTEM

Using a computer would be very tedious and time consuming if you had to know exactly how the CPU, memory, disks, etc., work and had to tell the CPU exactly how to operate each of the peripherals. Fortunately, programs have been written specifically to do those tasks. That set of programs is known as an *operating system*.

The operating system, or O.S., is the major group of system programs. As the name implies, an O.S. controls the operation of the system, both hardware and other software. It controls input and output, the peripherals, and the running of other programs. When the computer is turned on, an O.S. program controls the start-up procedure. When you type in a line of data for use by a program the O.S. controls the data transfer to that program. When you wish to operate a piece of hardware, you type in a rather general command which the O.S. understands (known as a *system command*), and the O.S. programs take care of all of the specific details required to operate the hardware. The O.S. is involved in every aspect of the computer's operation.

THE FILE MANAGER

Included with (or in) all operating systems is one or more programs known as a *file manager*. A *file* is a set of related information that has been stored on the computer as a single entity, similar to the office filing concept. In an office filing system, someone must be responsible for adding new files, removing old ones, adding to existing files, reordering files, making duplicates, locking certain drawers or cabinets, etc. Similarly, in the computer, the file manager programs allow you to build, purge, add to, rename, and copy files. They control the transfer of information to the CPU from the disk and tape units (and vice versa), and they control the printing of information. If there is more than one user, then the file manager also can control which user gets to look at what information.

TEXT EDITOR

At one time, computer programs were placed on cards, with one command per card. This was a long process, since a new card had to be placed into a typewriter-like device (called a keypunch) to do the punching and since a keypunching mistake could not be erased but required that the card be thrown away and a fresh one used. In some ways, though, the use of cards was helpful. If the programmer wanted to change a command line, then the appropriate card could be discarded and a new card re-punched. If several lines were out of place, their respective cards simply had to be removed and replaced in the proper order. If lines needed to be added, the new cards could punched and inserted at the appropriate places.

When entering a program into a computer, it is almost a certainty that you will make mistakes or wish to change the program at a later time. However, when changes have to be made, how do you do it? You cannot physically pull out a line and change it, but a system program is available which allows you to have the computer "pull" out a line and change it or replace it. The program which accomplishes this is called a *text editor*. Any computer which has an O.S. and a language translator will have some type of text editor to assist you in the entering and changing (editing) of programs.

Text editors come with different capabilities. Some allow portions of a line to be changed, but others require that an entire line be retyped, even if you only wish to change part of it. Many do not have the ability to move lines from one place to another, as could be done with cards. Some, however, have very sophisticated capabilities, including the ability to copy lines, to make the same change to several lines at one time, and to combine the lines from two different files (the same as taking two decks of cards and placing one behind the other). Any text editor will be sufficient for entering a program and making changes, but the latter is easier with some than it is with others.

COMPILERS AND INTERPRETERS

The CPU can execute simple adds, subtracts, multiplies, divides, compares, and jumps, known as *machine instructions*. These instructions required for the step-by-step operation of the CPU are very cryptic, consisting of binary patterns of 1s and 0s. It would be very tedious and time consuming to have to write all computer instructions in 1s and 0s, but at one time, computers were operated in exactly that fashion. Today, English-like commands (known as *source code*) have been developed that allow you to give the computer instructions in a simple, clear manner. These commands are found in the many *programming languages* which exist today, including BASIC, PASCAL, FORTRAN, COBOL, etc. However, the computer still "thinks" in 1s and 0s, so the source codes must be translated into machine instructions, or *machine code*. The translation process is similar to translating one spoken language to another, except that since the English-like commands are equivalent to several machine steps, each source code instruction is translated into several machine code instructions. Specially written programs, known as *compilers* and *interpreters*, exist that do the translation process for you.

A compiler and an interpreter differ in several ways. A compiler translates all of the commands in the source code program into their corresponding machine code instructions, creating a machine code program. Then the machine code program is executed to perform the task. An interpreter, on the other hand, translates and executes one source code command at a time. For instance, given the simple English program:

(1) Input a number

(2) If the number is less than 0, stop
(3) Input a second number
(4) Add the two numbers
(5) Print the sum
(6) Go back to the first instruction

a compliler would translate each instruction once, creating a machine code version, and then that version would be executed, with no need to return to the original source code version. An interpreter would translate the first instruction and execute it, then the second, then the third, fourth, fifth, sixth, and then it would go back and translate the first a second time before executing it, since it does not save any instructions as does the compiler. If the program continues to loop from step (6) to step (1) several times, then the interpreter is translating each statement several times and would take more time than a compiler to complete. Thus, the advantages of a compiler are: (1) each source code command is translated only once; (2) it requires less time to translate and execute a program with loops; and (3) since a machine code program is created, it may be stored on a disk or tape. Then the next time the program needs to be executed, the previously stored machine code version can be used, and no new translation is necessary. The advantages of an interpreter are: (1) it can detect an error as soon as a command is entered; (2) it allows the user to easily stop and start a program at any step and to quickly make and test changes; (3) it is just as fast or faster when used with simple, non-looping programs; and (4) an interpreter costs less. Also, less storage space is needed since only the machine instructions for one source code command at a time are present, rather than an entire machine code program. For these reasons, most personal computers are supplied with interpreters rather than with compilers.

System programs normally are supplied in machine code and therefore need not be translated. However, this means that you cannot read the code or change it (unless you know the binary instructions). Some computer manufacturers will provide the source code version, but usually at a higher cost. For the most part, don't expect to be able to alter the function of system programs.

USER PROGRAMS

User programs are those written or purchased by the user for a particular application (thus they also are called application programs). If they are purchased, they may not be in source code form. If they are, then you can make any changes to have the programs conform as nearly as possible to your specific application. If the are in machine code, then you will have to use them as is. As with system programs, the source code version will be higher priced than the machine code version (if both are available). In either case, if you are purchasing an applications program, it is best to find one fitting your needs, rather than attempting to make even slight alterations after purchase.

2. WHY SHOULD YOU BUY A PERSONAL COMPUTER?

In purchasing this Handy Guide, you probably already know why you *should* buy a personal computer. But you may not know the extent of either the capabilities or the requirements of a personal computer. This chapter will discuss the advantages and disadvantages in order to give you a more complete picture.

WHAT IT CAN DO FOR YOU

Personal computers are here to stay, and they are becoming more popular every day. All businesses, professionals, schools, and homes can find them useful. A computer, even the smallest one, is excellent for performing tasks of a repetitive nature, and it can remember and manipulate a great deal of information at one time. Once it has been correctly programmed to accomplish a task, you can be assured that it will arrive at the same results each time, with no miscalculations or, typographical errors (barring malfunctions, which are very rare). Through the addition of software which is designed to perform your desired application, you need only type in your data, and the computer will do the rest.

Some of the tasks for which a computer can be used in business environments include keeping track of finances, handling payrolls, completing tax returns, keeping an inventory, developing and maintaining a mailing list and generating form letters, word processing, and report generation.

In the professional environment, it can be used for calculating intricate mathematical, engineering, and accounting formulas, real estate analysis, keeping personal records, and report generation. A simulation software package can be written or purchased that will allow you to ask "what if?" questions for construction, scheduling, and purchases and have the computer provide the test procedure and results, thus saving money which would go for actual field tests.

In the field of education, it can give instruction in mathematics, science, spelling, foreign languages, and, of course, computer programming. And it can be used for keeping records of grades and in other administrative areas.

In the home, the personal computer can answer your telephone, instruct and entertain your children (and you), turn lights and appliances on and off at specified times, keep a household inventory, plan a budget, write letters, and so forth. More applications are being developed all the time.

As personal computers appear in more and more businesses, working establishments, schools, and homes, those that do not have one will be at a disadvantage. The speed, information retention, and accuracy of the computer are increasing productivity, lowering manufacturing costs, improving the educational environment, thereby increasing the efficiency of businesses, offices, and the home.

WHAT YOU MUST DO FOR IT

There are a few disadvantages, usually not mentioned, that you should be aware of when you buy a computer. Personal computers are not simple machines. They expect everyone to be just so. You will have to learn many system commands and how to load programs and data, and it all will have to be done precisely. And if you write your own programs, you will find that they must be very specific and precise—a computer will do EXACTLY as it is told, even if it is told incorrectly.

In addition, there are various environmental considerations, even for personal computers. You cannot allow the keyboard to get overly dusty, or it may result in incorrect characters being sent to the computer. When larger home appliances are turned on and off, it may cause a power fluctuation large enough to affect the computer's operation (some computers more than others—this depends on the computer's susceptibility to AC power line interference and its tolerance for below normal voltage levels). This problem can be corrected through the purchase of a power line conditioning unit which connects between the computer and the outlet. Also, you cannot let a powerful magnet come too close to the memory and storage devices or it may destroy (demagnetize) the stored information.

In addition, there often are added expenses. The base price of most computers may not give you a computer that immediately can be put to use. The only software usually included is the operating system and a BASIC interpreter (and maybe some games). You will have to write your own programs (which may take a great deal of time) or buy applications programs (which can be expensive). Also, a device for getting a paper-printed version of your data, output, and programs is usually not included. This is a necessity for many applications and can be more expensive than the computer itself.

Once you buy a computer, there always is the temptation to keep adding to it. The "base" price soon may be doubled or even tripled. Chapter 4 and the comparison tables in the final chapter will show how the base price of a computer compares with the final price for certain applications.

A word of caution: No matter what the application, if the information being kept in a computer is very important and not easily replaced, it is important to transfer that informaton at regular intervals, either from one storage device to another (from disk to tape) or to a printed copy for filing in a folder. In the event of a serious breakdown it's advisable to have a backup copy of information in the computer. A computer is a wonderful, time saving, efficient machine, but it can break, just like any other machine. There is a saying that sometimes proves true: "Live by the computer, die by the computer." The point is, *use* it, but don't *totally depend* on it.

WHY DO YOU WANT ONE?

This section will examine a few possible reasons for purchasing a computer, moving from the most to the least technical and costly. More specific discussion of some of the uses will be found in Chapter 4.

BUSINESS

Perhaps you are looking for a computer for business or professional purposes. As mentioned in the first section of this chapter, a computer is useful in a number of applications in these areas. A great deal of office work is repetitive in nature. Often the same monthly reports are typed twelve times a year, time cards have to be typed up every two weeks or so, letters have to be typed and retyped, the same tax forms are filled out each year, conferences must be planned—the list is endless. Each of these can be typed into a computer once and then altered, printed, and copied as often as desired. Daily schedules can be given to the computer and it will determine the best time for an office conference. Income, expenses, and other financial information can be entered into the computer. It can even make out your tax forms for you!

The computer can be used as an automatic calendar and date reminder. The dates and times for meetings, seminars, deadlines, birthdays, anniversaries, and so forth, can be entered, and the computer will give you a to-do list at the beginning of each day.

Crucial and often needed information can be entered into the computer, available for quick access and report generating at any time. Perhaps you are doing an important feasibility study concerning planned equipment or land purchase or a business take-over or the marketing of a new product. The computer can be used to analyze the available information, predict future trends, and generate a report summarizing it all. Information can be stored concerning clients, patients, business associates, employees, and relatives. Then it can order the information by name, type, or importance, print mailing labels, and generate form letters.

Any business which keeps an inventory can benefit from a computer. All inventory information can be entered into the computer, including name, cost, description, order number, reorder point, useful life, quantity, vendor, material, and so forth. The information can be manipulated in any manner desired; and periodic reports signaling lower quantities, calculating their total value, or just listing the items can be generated.

A computer is excellent for performing calculations, evaluating formulas, determining costs, and for any other numeric application. It's faster and more accurate than a human and doesn't get tired or blurry eyed.

EDUCATION

Perhaps you are a teacher or a school official who is looking into personal computers for use in your school. A personal computer is an exciting and fascinating way for children to learn. It can be used as a teaching aid in mathematics, English, foreign languages, typing, and in most any other area. And, of course, it's the ideal way to teach computer programming and theory. As more and more primary and secondary schools purchase computers, students will enter college computer and data processing courses with a higher level of training, and those without such a background will be at a disadvantage. And as computers become more a part of everyday life, it is becoming increasingly important to provide a general introduction to younger students. Of course, in these inflationary times, budgets seem to be getting cut rather than increasing. Thankfully, though, some computer manufacturers offer special rates to schools. And many manufacturers have developed educational programs, so that you will not have to do any (or at least, much) of your own programming. Also, someone in your faculty may own a personal computer and will be willing to offer assistance. Often, having a person familiar with a particular unit may be the most important reason to purchase the same unit. A local computer store or a manufacturer's representative can inform you of any special educational discounts and programs.

Keep the following points in mind if you are investigating the purchase of a computer for educational purposes. First of all, if you decide to purchase several computers for use in one classroom, I would suggest checking to see if they all can be connected to a master unit from which the teacher can monitor the use of the other units. This can also serve as a check for unauthorized use. Second, note that teachers initially may be very nervous using a computer. It is possible that the store or manufacturer can provide some training time for the teachers even before your own units arrive. Many computer stores offer free evening classes for their customers. Third, after purchase of the computers and as teachers become more familiar with them, uses can be suggested that might not have been considered before purchase.

Have a brainstorming session with those involved to come up with even more uses for your computers.

Computers also have other uses in the field of education. A computer is an excellent grade book. You can keep all of your grades stored on a disk or tape and then compute averages, medians, ranges, and even have the computer print graphs. Updates can be made quickly and cleanly, and listings are easily printed. Similarly, other administrative jobs and record keeping can be done with a computer.

If you are interested in learning computer programming, then a personal computer is an excellent and fun way of learning and of practicing what you are learning. If, however, you are interested in seeking a job as a programmer, you should seek formal instruction. There is much more to developing expertise in dealing with computers than just learning to write programs.

Perhaps you have children who have been pestering you for a computer, or you feel that a computer would be a good tool for instructing them in mathematics or spelling or some other field, or you want to get them started early in the very much-in-demand profession of computer programming. It's true that a computer can be very instructive for children. However, many parents who have purchased a personal computer with the hope of teaching computer programming to their children find that their children think of it as only a video game. If a computer is to be used only for playing games, then seriously consider a video game instead. But if you feel that your children are sincerely interested in learning about computers and about programming, and that you are serious in motivating and fostering that interest, then there is no better or more exciting way for them to learn than with their own computer.

GAMES

Perhaps you are interested in games. Perhaps, too, you would like to get into writing your own programs. If that is the case, you might consider one of the popular video games which later can be expanded into a computer. These machines have excellent computer games and will allow you to determine if that is really all you want. If not, then they can be expanded into full-fledged computers.

A computer can be an exciting toy and it can be a great conversation piece. If, however, those are the only reasons for purchasing one, perhaps a video game would be a more appropriate and less expensive alternative. There are a large number of cartridges available for some video game models, and the quality is equal to, if not higher than, that of the games found in personal computers. A computer is not a toy or simply a game machine and will not be as easy to use as one. You will have to learn several details concerning its operation—it is not operated by just flipping an on-off switch. I'm sure there are many personal computers sitting and collecting dust simply because people found they were more complicated than expected. Be sure you understand exactly what you are getting into.

HOW MUCH WILL IT COST?

Consider the purchase of a car. Let's say you want a functional, new car that has room for five, automatic transmission, air conditioning, power steering and a sun roof. You look at one model with a base price of $6,000. For this amount you get a car that is pretty much "stripped." The features you want are all optional extras that will add considerably to the base price, and a sun roof isn't even available. After shopping around, you find another model with a base price of $7,500 and the features you wanted are all standard (except for a sun roof, which is $300 extra). In addition, an AM/FM radio is included at no extra cost. Chances are the second model will be a better value for you.

The same goes for buying a personal computer. The base prices of personal computers vary greatly, but so do the features included. Almost every element of a computer will vary from model to model, including memory size, display, storage devices, and so forth. For instance, the Atari 800 and the TRS-80 Model III are fairly close in price, but the price of the TRS-80 includes a video display. The Atari does not but requires a separate T.V. or other video display. However, the Atari has color capability while the TRS-80 is black and white only. If the two machines were otherwise identical (which they definitely are not), someone who desires color and has a spare T.V. might choose the Atari; someone who does not want color or who does not have a color T.V. would be wise to choose the TRS-80.

How then should you determine how much to spend on a personal computer? First, *decide on what you want your computer to do.* This is the single most important step in choosing a personal computer. Then, find out what capabilities and features are needed to perform these tasks. To a large extent, these features will dictate the cost of the system you require.

If, for example, you need a new car to haul around a large trailer, then a 4-cylinder economy car will not do the job. You'll have to pay whatever it costs for a larger car or a pick-up truck. Likewise, if you want a personal computer to do (among other things) word processing, then you will need at least a good sized display and a quality printer. And chances are a computer that can only display 32 characters on a line will not serve your needs.

Furthermore, in considering the price of a computer include not only the features you need, but the software necessary to perform the desired functions. Don't think that you will be able to buy a computer, pick up a book, and write your own application programs. It takes even the most qualified programmers hundreds or thousands of hours to program any but the most simple tasks. And even if you can write your own programs, you have to consider the value of your time as a cost (unless you write programs for fun). The best way to meet your software needs is to buy "canned" or prewritten programs. Don't forget to include the cost of these programs when determining how much you will need to spend.

If you have a cost ceiling, then determine whether or not you can afford the computer you want. Perhaps you find that for all the applications you have in mind you'll need to spend $10,000 on a computer, peripherals, and software, and you have $3,000 in your budget. Either forget about buying a computer, or lower your expectations. See what functions can be performed for $3,000 and determine if they are sufficient to warrant the expense. It is usually possible to upgrade your system at a later date, adding features and software when you can afford them. If this is your plan, be sure that the system you purchase *can* be upgraded to meet all of your expected applications. Most personal computers have limitations on maximum memory size, which can limit their expandability. Also, note the cost of expansion. Some models include in the base price the connectors (interfaces) necessary for attaching printer or storage devices, but with some other models, the interfaces are extra.

In recent years computers have continued to drop in price, or have more features included at the old price. And new types are constantly appearing. (For example, today we have pocket computers which were not available a short time ago.) So the natural question is, "Shouldn't I wait until they drop in price?" If you really can't afford them at the present price, then yes, definitely wait awhile. But if you simply are waiting to get the most for your money, you may be in for a surprise. Some models do, indeed, drop in price, but some also increase in price. If you see a computer that you want and can afford it, it may be a good idea to buy it now. If the price rises, you will have made a wise choice; but even if it falls, you still will be money ahead if you are making use of your computer. Remember the calculators that you could purchase for $300 to $400 in the mid-seventies? Of course, you can get a computer for that price, now, but you have had five to six years of use from that calculator. Buy now or wait? The decision is yours.

3. CHOOSING A PERSONAL COMPUTER

This chapter will give you facts to consider, questions to ask, and features to check when choosing a personal computer. The final decision must depend on your own applications and your own personal taste.

WHAT FEATURES ARE IMPORTANT TO YOU?

When you're faced with the decision of choosing a computer you may be overwhelmed by the different types and features. This section will discuss several features found in personal computers and the advantages and disadvantages of each.

WHICH OPERATING SYSTEM?

The operating system controls all of the peripherals of the computer as well as other programs, so it is important to choose one that allows the use of the devices and software necessary for your applications. Some computers offer an O.S. that is simple to use but limited in its commands or in the types of hardware it can manipulate. But there may be another O.S. available as an option that, though more complicated in its commands, allows the user to attach more or different types of peripherals. For instance, one computer comes with an O.S. that can use only a cassette unit as a storage device. If you want to use a disk, then you have to purchase an optional O.S. Some computers have only one O.S. available. If you choose such a computer, then you will have to settle for what is standard. Some computers do not include an O.S. in the base price, but offer several from which to choose. There are certain O.S.'s that have been written for use by most any (but not every) computer with a particular CPU. For instance, the CP/M Operating System is written for use with several computers that contain an Intel 800 CPU (and extensions of those). This is a very popular O.S., and since it is compatible with so many computers, many other types of software have been written to work with the CP/M O.S.

CP/M

If a computer can make use of the CP/M operating system, then it usually can make use of the multitude of software packages that have been written for use with CP/M. I say "usually" because even though the software will run properly on the computer, it may not be available on diskettes or tapes which are compatible with that computer. When discussing disks and tapes earlier, it was mentioned that different models store different amounts of information (called *storage density*) per inch of tape or per a given area of a platter on a disk. Thus if computer A has a different disk storage density than computer B, then a floppy diskette from computer A will not work with a disk unit for computer B. There are companies which specialize in distributing CP/M software and they make it available for most computers using CP/M. Usually computers using CP/M will have a large supply of available software. The comparison tables in the final chapter list if CP/M is available.

ROM or RAM

For many personal computers, the operating system is included in ROM, the read only memory discussed in Chapter 1. In other personal computers, it is included on a diskette for use with a disk unit. There are advantages and disadvantages to both approaches. Since the CPU expects its instructions to be in memory, a computer which has the O.S. on disk must load the necessary instructions into RAM before they can be used. That means that some of the RAM will not be available for user programs and data, a definite disadvantage of the O.S. residing on disk. The advantage is that if you want to change the O.S. all you have to do is remove the first diskette and replace it with another that contains the second O.S. The disadvantage with having the O.S. in ROM is that it is more difficult, and sometimes impossible, to use a different O.S. Often the first ROM must be removed and a new one put in its place. Some computers circumvent this problem by placing the second O.S. on disk (as above) and then having the ROM O.S. give control to it immediately after start-up of the computer. The advantage of a ROM O.S. is that very little, if any, RAM needs to be used for storing the instructions.

Even though an operating system is a necessity (and it is important to choose the correct one), its choice usually depends on the other features that you want included in the computer. If you want a disk, then you have to choose an O.S. that works with a disk (usually called a *disk operating system* or *DOS*). If you want to use a certain programming language, then you need an O.S. that accepts the translator for that language. After you have determined the capabilities and peripherals you need for your application, it is time to find the operating system that will support them. Don't choose a computer and an operating system and then try to mold your application around them.

WHICH PROGRAMMING LANGUAGE?

Do you want BASIC, Pascal, COBOL, or Assembly? There are some excellent Handy Guides in this series available which examine the features of the most popular programming languages in some depth, but a few comments should be made here.

BASIC is the most popular programming language used with personal computers. It is a general all-around language, useful in most applications, since it easily handles mathematical equations and strings of characters (as in word processing). It normally is interpretive (translated by an interpreter) and therefore allows a program to be started and stopped at almost any statement. It also is an excellent language for beginning programmers since it will process a statement and point out any syntactical mistakes as it is entered. There are BASIC programs for most applications.

Some computers also provide compiler BASIC. The advantage here is that execution is faster (as explained in Chapter 1), providing speeds of three to five times that of an interpreter BASIC, depending on the application. However, the final two advantages of an interpreter as mentioned earlier are lost.

Pascal originally was developed for instructional purposes and is useful in teaching computer programming and theory. Recently, however, it has been growing in popularity faster than any other language, and is the second most popular programming language used with personal computers. Pascal has features of each of the languages being discussed as well as some special ones of its own. It has commands which make it very easy to manipulate numbers, characters, and words, making it useful in business, professional, and scientific applications. Using Pascal, a programmer can write a program which is much more understandable than in BASIC, and which is easier to debug (that is, find mistakes). It is the language of the future.

COBOL is a business oriented language. It is very popular for use with larger computers but is just beginning to appear in the personal computer field. It is excellent for business and file manipulation applications, but there are virtually no commercially developed COBOL programs for personal computers.

Assembly Language, a programming language available for several personal computers, is a simple language in which one assembly language instruction translates into one machine instruction. The assembly language commands allow the programmer to use the machine instructions without having to write them in 0s and 1s. Therefore a program written in assembly language must do the step-by-step procedure the CPU expects. Such a program is more time consuming to write, but it allows you to make use of the machine instructions exactly as you wish, rather than depending on a compiler or interpreter to choose the machine instructions. Having this choice allows you to write a program that makes very efficient use of the available machine instructions: a program that will execute in less time than an equivalent program written in one of the other languages. The variation of assembly languages is as wide as the types of CPU, since they mirror exactly a particular CPU's instruction set. The system program which does this one-to-one instruction translation from assembly language to machine language is called an *assembler*. As with a compiler, it assembles the entire program before beginning execution.

Some personal computers do not include any programming language translator, and, in fact, if you plan only to purchase pre-written software (usually referred to as a software *package*) which is in machine code, you will not need a language translator. If a translator is included with a computer, it usually will be a BASIC interpreter. If you wish to use a different language, it may not be available as an option. As with O.S.'s, programming language translators are available both in ROM and on disk, with the same advantages and disadvantages as those mentioned concerning O.S.'s.

When deciding which language to use, determine if you plan to purchase your applications software or write it yourself. If it is the former, first select the software you need, whatever the language, and then purchase the system and translator needed to run that software. If you plan to write your own software, then decide which language you prefer to use and which seems most oriented to your type of application. Any problem that can be solved in one programming language can be solved in another, but it may be harder or easier, depending on the language and the problem.

Once a language has been chosen which version should you choose? Even within a single line of computers, there may be two versions of a language. Some versions of BASIC will allow only integer numbers (whole numbers, such as 10, – 230, 0, 5000) while others will accept integer and real numbers (those with a decimal part, such as 5.54, – 18.2, 0.4). In other instances, one version of a language may have more commands available than another. If you plan to purchase your software, then you will want to choose the language version that supports that software. If you plan to write your software, then the choice of language version is primarily determined by your application. If your application is non-mathematical, then an integer-only language is fine. If it is financial programming, then a language with real numbers would be desirable. If you wish to do graphics, then you want a version which includes graphics commands. As with operating systems, first decide on your applications and then choose the appropriate language version.

HOW MUCH MEMORY?

Generally, there are two types of memory found in a personal computer. The first is referred to as RAM or random access memory (see the section in Chapter 1 for a more thorough discussion). This is the memory in which programs and data being used by the CPU are stored. On most systems, this is the primary limitation on program size, since usually the program running must be in memory in its entirety. Some systems start at 4K or 8K RAM, and that is enough for most hobbyists. If you are planning on business or other large programs, such as word processors, inventory control, or statistical analysis, or large amounts of data, then a system of 16K or larger will be necessary. By looking at the specifications of available programs (written in the same language and running on the same computer you would be using), you can get an idea of how much memory certain types of programs require. And many packaged programs will tell how much data can be handled with different amounts of RAM. Also, in Chapter 4, several applications will be presented with their usual RAM requirements. If your application allows it, then it is fine to start with a small amount of RAM, but note whether or not the amount of memory can be expanded and how much it will cost.

Unfortunately, with most computers, the total amount of RAM is not available to hold user programs and data. If the O.S. and/or language translator reside on disk or tape, then they will have to be placed into RAM along with the user programs. For example, if a computer has 32K bytes of RAM, but requires 27K bytes to hold the O.S. and translator, then only 5K is available for the user. When comparing computers, check how much *user* RAM is available and not just the total amount of RAM. In some cases, a computer with 32K bytes of RAM and its O.S. and translator residing in ROM will have more RAM available to the user than a computer with 48K bytes of RAM and its O.S. and translator residing on disk (thus having to be placed into RAM for execution by the CPU). The comparison tables in Chapter 5 include the amount of RAM occupied by the O.S. and translator for a few computers.

The second type of memory is ROM, or read only memory. This memory usually contains the operating system and a language interpreter. However, some computers have special slots for inserting the ROM modules containing applications programs (called cartridges). Such a procedure is more convenient than having to read a program from a disk or tape and it means you can use programs that might not fit into the computer's user RAM. Unfortunately, systems which have large ROM capacities usually have correspondingly lower RAM capacities, since there is a limitation on the total memory capacity. If you plan to purchase ready-made software in ROM form, this may not be a problem. But, even in that case, remember that you still may need RAM for data storage while a program is running. If a program expects its data to be in memory at all times (as some payroll programs do), then the amount of RAM will be the restriction on the quantity of data you can process (for instance, 16K might accept 40 employees whereas 4K would accept only 10). If you plan on writing all or most of your own software, then a large ROM capacity (and correspondingly lower RAM capacity) will be a detriment rather than an advantage.

DO YOU NEED A CASSETTE?

The lowest priced mass storage device is a cassette unit, and such a unit is standard with some personal computers. They are slow when compared to disks (a program requiring 16K of user RAM might take five minutes to load from a cassette and only a few seconds from a disk), but can make use of regular audio cassettes, and often a cassette tape recorder that you already own may be usable. But cassettes are sequential devices, meaning that to get to one location on the tape you must pass all other locations between it and your present location. Usually data can be stored only sequentially, and you cannot go back and enter extra information into an existing file since you may write over the next file on the tape (just as recording a song on the middle of a tape may erase part of the following song). If your application does not require random access or storage capabilities and you can tolerate the slower speeds, then a cassette might be suitable. If you are purchasing a disk unit in any case, then a cassette unit may not be necessary, and, in fact, some personal computers do not accept both a disk and cassette. But even with a disk unit, if a cassette unit can be connected, it would allow the purchase of programs at the lower price of cassettes, which then could be entered into the computer and transferred to a diskette. Also, some programs might be available only on cassette. In any case, a cassette unit is one of the least expensive additions to a computer system.

DO YOU NEED A DISK (OR TWO)?

Once you have used a computer with a disk unit, one which has only a cassette unit will seem slow and tedious. Transfer of information is much faster and easier with a disk. And unlike most tape units, disks allow you to access and write to a file in a random manner (that is, to non-consecutive records) and to add to the end of an existing file. Also, some computers allow a program larger than the available RAM to be divided into parts on a disk and then transfer each piece to RAM and execute as needed (this is known as *chaining* or *overlays*). If you have two disk units, then you can handle larger programs and amounts of data, and you can copy the information from a disk in one unit to a disk in the other unit (a process known as *backup*). But a disk unit is expensive (the least expensive units cost four to five hundred dollars) and requires more care than a cassette unit. If you really don't need one, you can save a great deal of money by purchasing a cassette unit instead. But you should check on the possibility of later adding a disk unit; it's possible that your needs and applications may change.

DO YOU NEED A PRINTER?

If a computer has a video display, there may be a need for a "hardcopy" paper *printer* for occasional printouts. A hobbyist probably won't need a printer, but, as with other features, it is important to know if the possibility of connecting a printer exists and the types that may be connected. Some computers come equipped with the hardware necessary for attaching a printer (called a *printer interface*), but most do not. The interface can usually be purchased separately.

For most purposes a printer is a necessity. The remainder of this section will discuss the pros and cons of the printer features mentioned briefly in the section on hardware in Chapter 1.

A comparison of most printers' features follows:

- UPPER CASE ONLY *VS.* UPPER/LOWER CASE
  If a printer is offered in both versions, then the upper case only version will be less expensive. Also, it may printer faster as the print mechanism has fewer possible characters to worry about. For many applications, such as statistical analysis, payroll, mailing lists, grading, inventory, and others, upper case only printing may suffice. For word processing, form letters, and a few others, it is desirable to have lower case letters also. In some instances, upper case printers have a few special characters missing also, such as , |, {, and }. Check if you need those, also. Study your application and determine if you really need the lower case capability. If not, you can save some money.
- 8½- X 11-INCH PAPER *VS.* 14- X 11-INCH PAPER
  The less expensive printers offer standard 8½- x 11-inch forms. This does not necessarily mean, however, that they are restricted to 80-column lines, since some have a compact mode of printing to allow 132 or more columns to be squeezed into 8½ inches. Of course, the compacted printing will be harder to read and will not be typewriter quality. Most applications need only 80 columns. If you really want 14-inch paper, you can expect to pay as much as $1,000 more than for an 8½-inch paper printer of similar quality.
- THERMAL *VS.* IMPACT
  Thermal printers use a special heat-sensitive paper and have a special print mechanism (or print *head*) that imprints on the paper. These printers are less expensive than impact printers (which make impressions on regular paper by impact, as does a typewriter) and may have more extensive graphics capabilities since the special print head allows for a wider range of characters than most impact print heads. The problems with thermal printers are that the paper is much more expensive (the price difference could be as

much as 1000%—$.10/sheet *vs.* $.01/sheet) and the paper tends to darken when exposed to light for long periods of time. Also, the thermal paper cannot give the appearance of a typewritten document. For temporary printouts or quick reports, a thermal printer will suffice. Also, the initial savings might offset the additional paper cost.

- MATRIX IMPACT *VS.* FULL FONT (OR FULLY-FORMED CHARACTERS
  The most popular and least expensive impact printers use a print head containing a matrix of printing dots each of which imprints depending on the character requirements. Fully-formed character printers have a print mechanism containing the entire form of the character. The latter type will give typewriter quality printout and is most suitable for word processing, though a few of the higher quality (and more expensive) matrix printers offer very good results. For most uses, the former type will suffice; it will save money and be faster. See Figure 3.1 for examples of matrix and full font characters.

Matrix Printing may be low
density for general uses,
or it may be high density
for word processing uses.

Some Matrix
Printers also allow the
use of different sized characters,
in both low and high density.

FULL FONT PRINTING CAN BE ALL
UPPER CASE AND OF RELATIVELY
LOW QUALITY, OR IT CAN BE OF

very high quality when using printers
suitable for word processing. These
printers also may provide more than
one character size if they have
interchangeable daisywheels or print
elements.

FIGURE 3.1 Printing examples from printers with different quality characters.

- PRINTER SPEED
  If your application requires speed more than typewriter quality, then you will want to choose a dot matrix printer or a thermal printer rather

than a full font printer. Common speeds for the latter range from 30 to 55 characters per second (cps). Dot matrix impact printers commonly range up to 180 characters per second. Thermal printers print at these speeds and higher.

- PROPORTIONAL SPACING *VS.* STRICT COLUMNS
  Many matrix printers and some full font printers allow the column spacing to be proportional. This gives the ability to produce newspaper-like printout, with even (*justified*) left and right margins. This is useful for some word processing and report applications. It is an added cost, though, and you should determine if you really need it.
- SINGLE SHEETS *VS.* CONTINUOUS FORMS
  Typewriters and a few typewriter-like printers allow only single sheets of paper rather than continuous forms. This is good for letters and applications that require a special letterhead, but the paper changing will get tiresome if your application requires long printouts. There are two types of printers that use continuous forms: those with sprockets (known as pin or tractor feed) and those without (known as friction feed). Paper with no sprocket holes (roll paper) is less expensive than that with holes, but the former tends to come in fewer types, as it is not used as often in large computer sites. Also, the lack of sprocket holes may allow the paper to slip, depending on the printer. Continuous forms with sprocket holes are the most common and come in many types. If you want your printout to have a typewriter quality, then you can trim off the sprocket holes after printing. Also to be considered when choosing a printer with sprockets is whether or not the distance between the sprockets is adjustable. If so, then a wide-carriage printer can use less expensive narrow forms when wider forms are not needed. This is desirable if a printer with a 14-inch width is purchased, so that standard 8½-inch paper also can be used. The best all-around printer is one that has adjustable sprockets for continuous forms but also allows for single sheet feeding.
- MISCELLANEOUS
  Can the printer print color or graphics? This is useful for reports or statistical applications. Also, can it handle carbon forms? What is the maximum number of copies? Keep these questions in mind when investigating printers.

DISPLAYS

TYPE

In Chapter 1, it was mentioned that some computers include a display and a keyboard and some do not. Of those that do not, some include the keyboard and require the user to supply the video display. Then there are those that do not include either. There are advantages to all three configurations. The first is a complete package and is more compact and simple for a beginner, the second allows a choice of video displays and the possibility of using a presently owned T.V., and the third allows the most choice and the possibility of purchasing a professional type CRT (cathode ray tube) *terminal* with display and keyboard.

A CRT is manufactured for use with most any computer, is relatively expensive (from $700 on up), and usually offers higher resolution and the capacity to display more characters at a time than the displays offered with a personal computer (except for a few of the more expensive personal computers). Also, a CRT is far superior to a T.V., for use as a display.

Another advantage of the second configuration that should be mentioned is that if a computer can be connected to a T.V., then you have a very transportable unit that can be attached to any T.V. at any location. But a word of warning—the higher quality the T.V., the higher quality the display (that is, the more crisp the characters and, if color, the cleaner the colors). Older and less expensive T.V.s may not give adequate results. That is why many computer companies offer specially manufactured television sets (known as *monitors*) that give results superior to those of a normal T.V. Be sure to check the quality of a display before purchase.

SIZE

If you are purchasing a computer that includes a display, it is important to choose one which you feel is large enough for clear viewing. If you are looking at a computer that connects to T.V.s you may not consider this paragraph to be important, since you can use a large-screen T.V. However, display size refers not only to the diagonal dimension of the screen, but also to the number of characters which can be displayed on the screen at any one time; and a larger display only enlarges the size of the characters, not the quantity of characters able to be displayed. The quantity is controlled by the computer. Some print 24 lines of characters on a display, but with only 40 characters or less per line; others print only 16 lines, but with 64 characters per line; and a few print 24 lines with 80 characters per line, the amount usually found on CRT terminals (a few provide 24 x 80 only when such a CRT terminal is connected). If you will be using your computer for word processing or letter writing, then it may be important to have a computer which provides at least 64 characters per line, if not the full 80 (the closer to the number of characters allowed on a normal typewriter, the better). With a computer that displays only 32 or 40 characters per line, you normally may type in more, but the line will be wrapped around to the next display line. This makes no difference to the computer, but it may make reading more difficult, especially if the break is in the middle of a word. However, the longer lines can be printed on a printer without wrap-around, if the printer supports their length.

COLOR OR BLACK AND WHITE?

The choice of color or black and white depends very much on what you will be doing with your computer. Color is more pleasing if you will be developing games or instructional programs. Also, most computer-generated graphs and charts are more meaningful when done in color. Black and white is adequate (if not preferable) for word processing, inventory, and financial planning. A computer that generates color will generally be more expensive and usually does not include the color display. Also, because of the more critical resolution requirements of color, these computers usually generate less characters per line (40) than a black and white computer (64). Finally, a color display may be more tiring on the eyes during long sittings. Personally, I have found the greenish (though still monochrome) displays available with some computers to be among the most pleasing to the eyes.

GRAPHICS

The graphics capability of a computer is an important feature to many people. Contrary to what you may think, graphics are important for serious pursuits as well as for games. You may wish to develop bar charts or time *versus* cash flow graphs. But whatever the application, if graphics capabilities are important to you, then be sure to consider several items.

First of all, there are two ways graphics can be displayed: using special symbols or blocks of light. The advantage of symbols is that they are preset forms which can be used quickly. The disadvantage is that you are limited to the symbols provided. The other approach allows you to treat the display as a checkerboard (or *matrix*) of squares that can be turned on (lightened) or turned off (darkened), or in the case of color graphics, colors can be changed, offering you a large number of different designs. The disadvantage is that it takes longer and you may not be able to produce certain special symbols with acceptable resolution (see next paragraph). The latter method is the most common since it allows the greatest variety of designs. Also, a few computers offer a combination of both and/or the ability to program your own special symbols.

Second, what is the *resolution* of the graphics? That is, what is the maximum number of positions vertically and horizontally which can be used in generating graphics? For example, a low resolution system might be only 32 x 64 positions and a high resolution system perhaps 240 x 540. The higher the resolution, the higher quality the graphics; that is, higher resolution means that diagonal lines and curves (and all non-horizontal and non-vertical lines) appear smoother and more natural.

Third, can graphics be interspersed with alphanumeric text? This is important for labeling axes and charts, for example. This capability usually exists, but be sure to check.

Other than these, the best judge of graphics is your own eye and taste. What you like the best may be the most important factor.

KEYBOARD RELATED FEATURES

The type and layout of the keyboard, and related computer features, can be very important in your computer applications. A primary question to ask is, "Does the keyboard (and computer) have lower and upper case letters?" Many personal computers have upper case only (with a few of those offering a lower case option). If your application requires lower case (say, word processing), then limit your shopping to those models. A few will allow lower case to be sent to a printer but display only upper case on the video monitor; for some applications, that may be sufficient, but it could get confusing.

Another important feature to check is if the keyboard allows touch-typing speeds. Each time a key is pressed on the keyboard, the corresponding character is sent to the CPU. During this transmission, the keyboard is prevented from sending any more characters (even though you can press the keys, nothing will be received by the computer nor appear on the display). If the CPU responds rather slowly in accepting the characters, then it may not "unlock" the keyboard before you have typed another key. If that happens, then that character will not be sent to the CPU and you may get something like the following.

```
Nw is te time foral good me tocome to te . .
```

rather than:

```
Now is the time for all good men to come to the . .
```

In other words, you will have to slow down to match the character transmission speed of the computer. If a computer will accept characters as fast as you can type them in, it has what is known as "'n-key rollover." This is an important feature if you are a fast typist. The easiest way to test for this is to sit down and type some familiar lines as fast as you can. You will soon know whether or not the computer can keep up.

If you will be purchasing your applications software, the documentation that comes with the packages may refer to *control characters* or *Control Key* (this quite often is the case with word processing software). A control character is a non-printing character that is used for special purposes, such as sending characters to random locations on a display (as opposed to a normal line by line sequence) or causing a printer to print in a compressed mode. A control key is a special key on the keyboard (often labeled "CNTL" or "CTRL") that is used in conjunction with the other keys to generate control characters. For instance, if the control key and the "A" key are pressed simultaneously, the computer is sent a "Control-A" character. Not all personal computers have such a key, but those without one have software available that works without it. If the software that you wish to use does require one, be sure to check for it as you look at the various models of computers. If you are familiar with computers and will be doing your own programming, you probably have used a control key and may want to have one on your personal computer.

If you are accustomed to certain types of typewriter keyboards, you may want to choose a computer with a similar layout and structure. And even if you are not accustomed to typing, you still should note such things. Some computer keyboards have their non-alphanumeric characters in rather unusual locations, which may cause confusion. Some keyboards have their keys in a straight horizontal and vertical layout or in a reduced area, and, though this may not seem important to a new typist, the standard-sized offset typewriter keyboard will be more desirable as you grow in your typing skill. Still other keyboards have no raised or separate keys but rather a flat touch-sensitive one. This type usually is safe from dirt and dust that can affect a normal keyboard, and is less expensive; however, exact finger placement is more difficult (especially, if you normally type without looking at your fingers). Moreover, the lack of the "feel" of a normal keyboard may bother some people.

You also might want to consider a few other keyboard features. For instance, if you are accustomed to typing numbers on a ten-key calculator keyboard, then the inclusion of a numeric keypad would be of interest to you. If quick access to graphic symbols is important, you might want to look at computers whose keyboards have graphic symbols directly accessible through using the normal keys in a different mode. Take time to try the keyboard and see if it feels comfortable and suits your applications.

OTHER FEATURES

There are many other features and attachments that may be of interest. Some of the more common ones include the following.

INTERFACES

Rather than having to develop your own connecting cables for attaching peripherals to the computer (as we did with the calculator in Chapter 1), standard device interfaces have been developed for this purpose. The RS-232C and the IEEE-488 are the most common industry standard interfaces and allow the use of a wide variety of equipment. The RS-232C is the most used and allows the connection or terminals, some printers, other computers, and other equipment. It is an important interface to have included (or available as an accessory). The IEEE-488 is used mainly for the connection of measurement and scientific equipment, but recently it has become increasingly popular for the connection of the more common peripherals such as those mentioned above. It is important to have at least one of these interfaces included or available as an accessory.

MODEMS

Many personal computers can be made to talk to other computers across telephone lines. This requires an RS-232C interface and a telephone acoustic coupler. Some personal computers have an RS-232C interface builtin, but on most it is an option. Acoustic couplers are not builtin on any personal computers, but must be purchased separately.

Acoustic couplers (also known as modems) come in three types: answer only, allowing another computer to call yours, originate only, allowing yours to call a computer with a modem with answer capability, and answer/originate, allowing the computer to receive and call. The term "originate" refers to a modem's ability to send a start-of-communications' tone. The modems with only "answer" capability can respond to that initial tone but cannot initiate the process. Also, a few modems with originate capability have autodial capabilities, so you can program it to dial a commonly used telephone number. Modems can be purchased from several sources, including a few of the computer manufacturers.

INFORMATION NETWORKS

There are many large computer installations that have special dedicated phone lines allowing dialing in by outside users. The user must have a valid identification name or number and a corresponding password. A personal computer can be connected to one of the computer information networks being developed for this purpose. These networks provide information services, news, business software, games, interaction with other users, and other features, all for a set rate per minute or hour of connect time. The network may be nationwide, but usually either a local phone number or a toll-free number is available. This capability gives the small computer user access to the computing power and features of a large computer system. Some of the most popular networks at present are MicroNET, The Source, and CompuServe. As of this writing, the costs for each of these is $5.00/hour, $2.50/hour, and $5.00/hour, respectively. If you seriously consider using such a network, check for the interest information on the services offered by each one you consider. (Since the services are always being updated, it would do little good to expound on them in this booklet.) For an all-news service, some newspapers now offer electronic news for off-hour headlines and/or access to past newspapers. Check with your local newspapers for information on this service.

SOUND

A feature of interest to many people—especially those who wish to write game programs—is a computer's ability to produce sound. Many have special commands or BASIC statements that make it quite easy to produce tones, add sound to a program, or even compose a song. These computers have either a built in speaker or make use of the speaker in the T.V. But even if a computer doesn't have special tone-producing commands, it may be able to produce sound. Any computer that accepts a normal audio cassette recorder as a mass storage device will transfer information using tones, with different tones used for different types of information. With many of these computers, it is a simple matter to write a program that appears to the computer to be transferring information, but that actually is producing tones through the speaker of the recorder. Of course, this method is not as easy or as sophisticated as builtin commands and probably would not be suitable if sound is an important consideration.

SPEECH

For certain applications, it may be desirable to have a speech synthesizer (so the computer can talk) and/or a voice recognizer (so you can talk to it). These are available for several models. (The speech synthesizer for the TI 99/4A is one of the best since it has entire words preprogrammed rather than requiring the combining of phonetic sounds to form words.)

An authentic sounding speech synthesizer can make a computer appear much friendlier to nervous users. With it, the computer can verbally correct or commend the user. This is especially useful in education. A speech synthesizer combined with a braille keyboard would allow a blind person to do much of what a sighted person could do with a computer.

Voice recognizers are in the early stages of development and really are only for experimentation. They can process only a few words and can be fooled by inflection and accent.

HOME APPLIANCES

Some personal computers accept attachments for controlling home appliances. The devices for controlling appliances allow you to connect an appliance to each controller; that appliance can then be turned on or off at preprogrammed intervals. If a thermostat or other external sensor were connected to the computer, it could determine itself when to turn certain devices on or off.

SECURITY

The devices for a security system allow you to connect a sensor to a window or door or other point of entry, and the computer can then maintain surveillance of the point of entry. If the surveillance sensor is triggered, the computer can sound an alarm, signal you, or even call the police using an autodialing model.

GAMES

If you are planning to write arcade-type game programs, you should look for a computer that will accept game playing devices such as joysticks since many computers do not have such devices.

HARDWARE EXPANSION

In the section on features, it was mentioned several times that you should note whether or not there was the possibility of adding certain items. Sometimes finding that information is not as easy as it sounds. Some attachments may not be available from the computer manufacturer, but they may be available elsewhere. There are many companies that do not make computers but specialize in attachments for those already available (especially the more popular models). Specialized devices, such a those mentioned in the previous section, may be available only from such a company. These companies may offer devices that also are offered by the computer manufacturer, but that are much less expensive since they do not carry the original manufacturer's brand name (RAM modules, called "chips" and disk units are notable examples). If that is the case, then you may wonder, "Why not save money and buy from the other company rather than from the computer manufacturer?" There are several possible disadvantages to this:

(1) The quality and (especially) the compatibility may not be up to that of equipment from the original manufacturer who makes the computer and knows its requirements better than anyone else.

(2) If the computer is still under warranty, the attachment of certain "unauthorized" pieces of hardware (notably RAM chips) may invalidate the warranty.

(3) If the computer should require servicing, then evidence that it has been tampered with may raise the service cost.

(4) If a problem occurs in the interfacing of the original equipment and the attached device, each company may point the finger and say it is being caused by the other company's equipment, and you will be stuck in the middle.

(5) If you update your computer in the future, devices from other companies may not function with the new version.

If you wish to connect a device to your computer that is not available from the original manufacturer, and the above points do not apply or are not important to you, then it is reasonable to purchase the device elsewhere. Even then you should talk with a representative of the computer manufacturer to determine the device's suitability. And, above all, either test for compatibility before purchasing the device or arrange for a test period with the option to return the device if compatibility fails. In performing the test, carefully follow the directions with both the computer and the device. Make sure you can make use of all the stated features and capabilities of the device. Some devices require a special program to be loaded into memory before the device can be used. If this is the case, check your present programs to see if they will run with that special program also loaded into memory.

SOFTWARE AVAILABILITY

The original manufacturer will have a certain amount of software available, but the amount is usually rather limited. However, especially for the more popular computers, a great deal of software is available from other sources. The Radio Shack TRS-80 has had, by far, the largest amount of software developed for it of any personal computer. The Apple and Commodore PET computers also have had a large amount developed. Other newer or less popular computers have less available. But a good deal of software has been developed for computers with CP/M operating systems. If the amount and types of software available is important to you, do some investigating before you buy.

Do the points above apply to software from an outside source? Numbers (1), (4), and (5) do apply, but they are not quite as crucial with software as with hardware. First of all, software usually is less expensive than hardware. Second, the programs can be changed as necessary (if you purchase source code). Third, computer manufacturers often sell their software only on an "as is" basis, with no warranty whatsoever, while many independent software producers actually supply a lifetime warranty. Warrantied software eliminates all points of the previous section except (5), and it may not apply to your situation.

SUPPORT AND SERVICE

The company or store from which you purchase your computer is as important as which computer you purchase. Sooner or later you may have questions or problems, or you may want to add new equipment, and it is important to have someone nearby to help. If you order your computer by mail to save money, it still is important to find stores nearby that can help you. If not, you may wait a long time to receive answers to your questions, and if you have to send your computer through the mail for servicing, it could be very expensive. It also is important to check on the financial status of the company that manufacturers the computer and the store that sells it. If either of these run into problems in the near future, you may be left with a computer that is very difficult to upgrade or to get serviced. How popular is the computer you are considering? If it is not a popular model, the manufacturer may drop it from its line and then service may be very difficult and upgrading impossible.

A certain amount of home maintenance can be done on computers and related equipment. Cleaning of the keyboard, print heads, cassette unit read/write heads, and the computer work area should be a regular procedure. If recommended by the manufacturer, disk read/write heads also should be cleaned periodically, but carefully follow all procedures, because the disk heads are very delicate and expensive. Following set procedures, such as turning off the computer and any peripheral before connecting or disconnecting them, can make your life with the computer much easier. But if a piece of hardware should break, there is little chance of servicing it yourself (unless you have an Electrical Engineering degree. If you make an attempt at self-service and fail, it may result in a higher service cost or even in the refusal by the manufacturer to service the equipment. A few manufacturers have a flat service fee for given pieces of *untampered-with* hardware; however, for the most part, service costs are high, averaging $60.00 per hour of service time. If you want on-site service then expect to pay travel expenses also. And even when you take or send the equipment out, there may be a set minimum (say, $100.00) for the service.

Most hardware has a 90-day warranty, though sometimes it may be up to a year. This allows a break-in period for the hardware, giving you time to run it through its paces. After that initial period, a service contract may be purchased from the manufacturer and/or the dealer, or perhaps from another party dealing primarily in service. The contract has a monthly or yearly cost proportional to the value and projected service requirements of the hardware. The yearly cost, which covers any service (other than that necessary because of abuse) and also may include the periodic maintenance, often is roughly equivalent to the cost of one major servicing. It also assures that the company will meet your needs before those of anyone without a service contract.

Do you need a service contract? It depends on several considerations. First of all, can you afford the monthly or yearly charges? If not, you might be better off taking a chance with no contract. Is the particular equipment (or the manufacturer) known for reliability? If so, you might not need a contract. Is the product fairly new? If so, you might want a contract, since all the "bugs" might not be out. Is there a flat service charge for the equipment? If so, a service contract would gain you very little. Is the replacement cost fairly close to the service contract cost over, say, a three year period? Then it might be better to save the money and built a reserve for a replacement rather than to spend it on servicing the present unit. With the ever-improving technology, replacement costs for computer equipment usually will go down. If you are using the equipment for a business, then you might want to consider when it will be fully depreciated. Perhaps a service contract only for the early life of the equipment would be an acceptable compromise.

4. SYSTEM REQUIREMENTS FOR SPECIFIC APPLICATIONS

This chapter examines various applications and discusses the hardware and software needs of each. Prior to looking at specific applications, however, a few general comments should be made. Before purchasing a computer or an applications programs package, list all of your objectives in making the purchase. Fully understand your requirements and how you want them fulfilled. What exactly do you want the computer to do? How do you want the final output to look? How will that output be used and by whom? Salespeople can help you solidify your needs, but they may misunderstand them and unknowingly lead you the wrong way. Their main job is to lead you to the right equipment *after* you have presented your needs. And if you don't have a list of specifics, then you may not be able to determine if the package they are presenting is satisfactory.

Determine also how simple you want to keep the new system or package. Some applications can be met in many ways, some easier than others; and some computers and software packages are easier to use than others. Do not take the first solution that you find. Look at it carefully, have it demonstrated, and try using it yourself. Then consider how much training you will have to undergo. When it comes to computers, there are many means to the same end.

Finally, it is possible that no single software package, or even combination of packages, will meet your needs exactly. You may have to take the one that comes closest and accept the weak spots. Software packages must have a certain amount of generality in order to be marketable. If the best one you find is not good enough, then you may have to go to a vendor who provides a software development service. They can develop a package geared to your unique requirements, but expect it to be expensive. Current programmer fees are around $50 an hour, and it will take hundreds or thousands of hours to develop any but the smallest applications programs.

WORD PROCESSING

Word processing is one of the faster growing applications of personal computers. Basically, word processing is using the computer to do that which would be done with a typewriter. However, the computer allows all of the editing, erasing, copying, and printing to be done on a video display, thereby eliminating the manual erasing, the use of white-out, the re-typing of entire documents (or pages), and the wasting of paper. The word processing system allows for the moving of entire paragraphs (or pages), quick deletion and insertion of words or lines, the storing of the document for later reuse, multiple copies, and, depending on the computer and printer, the capability to produce professional printer results with the right margins as well as the left margins lined up.

There are computers outside the realm of personal computers that are designed specifically for word processing. These word processing "systems" offer very sophisticated capabilities, including automatic hyphenation, spelling checks, and typesetting quality output. Such computers usually start at around $7,000. Personal computers can be used for word processing when combined with the appropriate software and hardware, but since they are designed for more general uses, they may or may not provide capabilities equal to those found in word processing systems. The following will discuss what is required when using a personal computer for word processing. Further study, including looking at the latest copy of each model's word processing instructions manual, would be useful in order to determine which provides the capabilities you require.

The basic system hardware requirements for word processing are the computer, a disk or cassette unit if storing of documents is desired, a keyboard, a video display, and a printer. The amount of memory, the quality of printer, and the type of data storage (disk or cassette) all are dependent on your application. If you plan to do no more than writing letters, then 16K RAM (or even 8K), a cassette unit (or none if all documents are for one-time use and the system accepts ROM software), and a standard quality matrix printer probably might suffice. If you are generating business reports, then you may want 48K or 64K, a disk unit or two, and a typewriter quality printer. Remember to consider the largest possible document you will be creating and then determine if the system can handle it (the maximum number of characters in any document cannot exceed total disk or cassette storage space minus area occupied by the system and word processing software). The software requirements are an O.S. to control the required hardware (as is required for all applications being presented) and a word processing software package designed to run under that O.S. The following is a typical configuration for business word processing:

$3,000–$5,000 System—
- 64K RAM minimum
- Standard keyboard w/function keys
- 12" Black & White display
- Dual 5¼" or 8" floppy disk units
- Letter-quality printer
- Word processing software

MAILING LIST

A mailing list is often included in a word processing software package. Such a system allows the storage of names, addresses, and other related information, the generation of mailing labels using the stored information, and, if used with a word processing package, the storage and usage of form letters.

The system requirements for a mailing list application are similar to those of word processing, and identical if the two applications are to be integrated. The systems listed above simply would need to have mailing list software added to their configurations.

ELECTRONIC WORKSHEETS

These programs made popular by the VisiCalc software package, are used for modeling and forecasting, acting as balance sheets and allowing the asking of "what if?" questions. They can be used in many applications, including sales analysis, budget planning, engineering process models, statistical analysis, and real estate. They work by entering numerical values and formulas, and defining relationships between the various rows and columns of values. Computations can be made and modifications of one or more values will show the respective effects on other values. When you have results you wish to list, they can be sent to a printer. VisiCalc and SuperCalc, by far the most popular systems, are available for several computers. Below is a possible configuration.

$1,000–$2,000 System—
64K RAM minimum
Single 5¼" floppy disk unit
Dot matrix printer
(Use present TV for display)
Electronic worksheet software

BUSINESS

Business and accounting applications are among the major uses of personal computers. These applications may include cash flow analysis (VisiCalc could be very useful in many accounting applications), payroll, general ledger, depreciation and interest calculations, inventory control, and accounts receivable and payable. Software for some of these applications may be purchased as separate software packages, but many are found in larger, more comprehensive, accounting or financial packages. Depending on the extent of the package, memory requirements may range from 4K RAM (yes, there are payroll programs which require only 4K RAM) to 64K; and mass storage requirements could range from a simple cassette to two or more 8" floppy disks. The type of printer would depend on who would be using the generated reports, with a typewriter quality printer being desirable for a more professional look. Special hardware may be necessary for some applications. The possible hardware and software combinations in this area are almost endless, but those listed below will provide a general idea of what is available.

It is possible that your application may require more than a personal computer can provide. Most personal computers are meant to be used by one person at a time. A few can handle multiple users through additional terminals, hard disks, and special operating systems, but it is important to test such a configuration before buying. A computer that is very fast with one user may become very slow with several users. The maximum simultaneous number of users usually is five. If, for any reason, you wish to have several terminals located at various points in a warehouse or office building and have them all connected to the same computer for access to the same data, then it may be necessary to go to a "business" computer. A personal computer may not allow enough terminals to be connected or it may not provide satisfactory speed under such heavy use. Similarly, most personal computers do not allow several programs to run at once. If you need access to a large amount (over 500,000 characters) of data, then a computer with a large storage hard disk is a necessity. A few personal computers accept hard disks, but the sizes available may not be sufficient. Consider the total possible characters required at any one time and then compare that value to the bytes of storage available (minus the storage required by the system and applications programs). Finally, if you require very high speed printers (say, 1200 lines per minute), you will have to go to a larger computer. Such printers are readily available for many "business" computers but not for personal computers.

PERSONAL FINANCE

Using a personal computer for financial applications in the home, for receipts and planning tax returns and budgets, requires much less equipment than a business application. These home applications usually require no more than a cassette unit and 16K, though a disk unit (and perhaps additional memory to be used with it) would be useful if additional speed and convenience were desired. A thermal printer would suffice for occasional printouts for your records (as long as the printout is not exposed to direct light for hours at a time). Below is a sample system.

$500 System—
- 16K RAM minimum
- Tape cassette unit
- Thermal printer
- (Use present TV for display)
- Personal finance software

COMMUNICATIONS

When you wish to communicate with a friend or a business associate, it is a simple matter to pick up a phone and call them, or, if close enough, to talk to them in person. Similarly, given the appropriate hardware and software, your personal computer can communicate with another computer. The first hardware requirement is an interface to connect the two computers. This usually is an RS-232C interface, but an IEEE-488 or other interface might be used if accepted by both computers. If the computers are close together (within the length of the interface cable), then no further hardware is required. If, however, they are farther apart, then the computers can communicate across a telephone line using a modem. In this case, the interface would connect to the modem and the modem would connect to the telephone line. There are many types of modems available, and it is not uncommon to purchase a modem which is not marketed by the computer manufacturer. In fact, many of the manufacturers do not market modems, but rather suggest models from other manufacturers. The manufacturers of the systems listed below, however, do market modems. Communications software also is required by your computer. This allows the personal computer to appear as a terminal to the other computer, but to retain the power of a computer, allowing it to run programs, store information, etc.

5. COMPARISON TABLES OF PERSONAL COMPUTERS

The comparison table of personal computers is not exhaustive in its list of computers nor in its list of features. If you are particularly interested in *portable computers* we refer you to the Handy Guide, *How to Buy a Portable Computer*. However, a few of the more popular portables are included. For each of the computers listed, the table summarizes a base price system, high-lighting the features discussed in Chapter 3. A range rather than an exact amount is given for each system's price because of the fluctuation in prices and the differences depending on the location of purchase. The order of the systems roughly represents their relative prices, with the least expensive coming first in the list.

The following remarks should be kept in mind as you look at the table. Any computer that has the capability to produce color on a display also may be used with a black and white display. The amount of RAM listed is the total amount and it all is not necessarily available to the user. If a computer has its O.S. and programming language translator in ROM, then most of the RAM will be available. If they are on disk, then as much as 32K of the RAM may be needed for them when they are being executed. The storage comments refer to the availability of a tape unit, disks or cartridges for the loading and storage of programs. Sometimes just an interface (not the actual unit) is included in the base price. The printer comments also refer to the presence of an interface or of an actual unit. All of the comments concerning specific hardware included with, or available for, the system refer to equipment available from the manufacturer. It does not imply availability or lack thereof from independent companies. This table is only a guide; for in-depth study, the latest literature from each manufacturer should be obtained.

I hope that this Handy Guide has been helpful in adding to your knowledge of computers in general, and personal computers in particular. Whether you plan to purchase a personal computer for your office, your business, or your home, you can now feel better prepared to make your choice.

PERSONAL COMPUTER MANUFACTURERS

Apple Computer, Inc.
10260 Bradley Drive
Cupertino, California 95014

Atari, Inc.
1265 Borregas Avenue
Sunnyvale, California 94086

Commodore Business Machines
487 Devon Park Drive
Wayne, Pennsylvania 19087

Compaq Computer Corp.
12330 Perry Road
Houston, Texas 77070

Digital Equipment Corp.
146 Main Street
Maynard, Massachusetts 01754

Fortune Systems Corp.
1501 Industrial Road
San Carlos, California 94070

Franklin Computer Corp.
7030 Colonial Highway
Pennsanken, New Jersey 08109

Hewlett-Packard
1820 Embarcadero Road
Palo Alto, California 94303

IBM Information Systems
Post Office Box 1328
Boca Raton, Florida 33432

Kaypro
Non-Linear Systems, Inc.
Post Office Box N
Del Mar, California 92014

Morrow Designs
600 McCormick Street
San Leandro, California 94577

North Star Computers, Inc.
14440 Catalina Street
San Leandro, California 94577

Osborne Computer Corp.
26500 Corporate Avenue
Hayward, California 94545

Otrona Corp.
2500 Central Avenue
Boulder, Colorado 80301

Sinclair Research
50 Staniford Street
Boston, Massachusetts 02114

Tandy Corp.
Radio Shack
One Tandy Center
Fort Worth, Texas 76102

Texas Instruments, Inc.
Post Office Box 73
Lubbock, Texas 79408

Vector Graphic, Inc.
500 N. Ventu Park Road
Thousand Oaks, California 91320

Victor Business Products
3900 North Rockwell
Chicago, Illinois 60018

Zenith Data Systems
1000 Milwaukee Avenue
Glenview, Illinois 60025

HARDWARE →

SYSTEM FEATURES	BASE PRICE	CPU TYPE	MEMORY (BYTES) RAM Standard Maximum	ROM Standard Maximum	STORAGE	PRINTER (Unit or Interface)	DISPLAY SIZE (DIAGONAL) Lines x Chars	COLOR OR MONO-CHROME	KEYBOARD LAYOUT U/L CASE	GRAPHICS TYPE RESOLUTION	RS232 INTERFACE	SOUND CAPABILITY STANDARD
TIMEX/ SINCLAIR 1000	under $50	Z-80A 8-bit	2K 16K	8K 8K	Includes Cassette Interface	Interface Included	Not Included Depends on Display 24 X 32	Mono-chrome	Non-Standard Membrane Uppercase	24 Graphics Characters (Matrix optional)	Not Available	No
COMMO-DORE VIC20	under $100	6502A 8-bit	5K 32K Total add-on RAM and ROM cannot exceed 28K	16K 43K	Includes Cassette Interface Optional Floppy Disks Accepts ROM Cartridges	Interface Included	Not Included Depends on Display 22 X 33	Color	Standard Both	Matrix 176 x 184 16 Colors	Not Included	Yes
ATARI 600XL	under $200	6502C 8-bit	16K 16K	24K 24K	Includes Cassette Interface Optional Floppy Disks Accepts ROM Cartridges	Interface Included	Not Included Depends on Display 24 X 40	Color or Mono-chrome	Standard Both	Matrix and Symbols 320 x 192 128 Colors	Optional	Yes
RADIO SHACK TRS-80 COLOR COMPUTER	under $200	MP6809E 8-bit	16K 32K	8K 32K	Includes Cassette Interface Optional Floppy Disks Accepts ROM Cartridges	Interface Included	Not Included Depends on Display 16 X 32	Color	Non-Standard Uppercase	Matrix 256 x 192 8 Colors	Included	Yes

	HARDWARE (cont.)			SOFTWARE →								
SYSTEM FEATURES	GAME PLAYING DEVICES AVAILABLE	SPEECH DEVICES AVAILABLE	HARDWARE EXPANSION	OPERATING SYSTEM	STANDARD CP/M AVAILABLE	WORD PROCESSING SOFTWARE AVAILABLE	ELECTRONIC SPREAD-SHEET	PROGRAMMING LANGUAGES INCLUDED	PROGRAMMING LANGUAGES AVAILABLE FROM MANUFACTURER	SOFTWARE AVAILABILITY	SERVICE AND SUPPORT	NOTES
TIMEX/ SINCLAIR 1000	Available from outside sources	No	Not too much available	Included in ROM	No	No	No	Extended BASIC in ROM	None	Some through Sinclair and elsewhere	Through Sinclair, by mail	Very inexpensive and very compact.
COMMO-DORE VIC20	Yes	No	Fair through Commodore	Included in ROM	No	Yes	No	BASIC in ROM	Assembler	Excellent game selection, some other through Commodore	Good through Dealers	Inexpensive and backed by successful manufacturer.
ATARI 600XL	Yes	Yes	Excellent through Atari and elsewhere	Included in ROM	Yes	Yes	Yes	Atari BASIC in ROM	Assembler, Pilot, Microsoft BASIC, LOGO	Good through Atari, excellent elsewhere	Good through Dealers and Authorized Service Centers	An improved version of the successful 400 model.
RADIO SHACK TRS-80 COLOR COMPUTER	Yes	No	Some through Radio Shack	Included in ROM	No	Yes	Yes	BASIC in ROM	Extended BASIC, Assembler, LOGO, Pilot	Good through Radio Shack	Good through Dealers and Computer Centers	Inexpensive with the promise of future expandability.

HARDWARE →

SYSTEM FEATURES	BASE PRICE	CPU TYPE	MEMORY (BYTES) RAM Standard Maximum	MEMORY (BYTES) ROM Standard Maximum	STORAGE	PRINTER (Unit or Interface)	DISPLAY SIZE (DIAGONAL) Lines x Chars	COLOR OR MONO-CHROME	KEYBOARD LAYOUT U/L CASE	GRAPHICS TYPE RESOLUTION	RS232 INTERFACE	SOUND CAPABILITY STANDARD
TIMEX/ SINCLAIR 2068	under $200	Z-80A 8-bit	72K 72K	24K 56K	Accepts both Cassettes and ROM Cartridges	Interface Included	Not Included Depends on Display 24 X 64	Color	Standard Uppercase	Matrix 512 x 192	Optional	Yes
ATARI 800XL	under $300	6502C 8-bit	64K 64K	24K 24K	Includes Cassette Interface Optional Floppy Disks Accepts ROM Cartridges	Interface Included	Not Included Depends on Display 24 X 40	Color or Mono-chrome	Standard Both	Matrix and Symbols 320 x 192 128 Colors	Optional	Yes
COMMO-DORE 64	under $300	6510 8-bit Z-80 optional	64K 64K	20K 20K	Includes Cassette Interface Optional Floppy Disks Accepts ROM Cartridges	Interface Included	Not Included Depends on Display 25 X 40 (80 cols. opt.)	Color	Standard Both	Sprite Matrix 320 x 200 16 Colors	Not Included	Yes
ATARI 1200XL	under $1,000	6502 8-bit	64K 64K	10K 24K	Includes Cassette Interface Optional Floppy Disks Accepts ROM Cartridges	Interface Included	Not Included Depends on Display 24 X 40	Color	Standard Both	Sprite Matrix 320 x 192 256 Colors	Included	Yes

HARDWARE (cont.) | SOFTWARE →

SYSTEM FEATURES	GAME PLAYING DEVICES AVAILABLE	SPEECH DEVICES AVAILABLE	HARDWARE EXPANSION	OPERATING SYSTEM	STANDARD CP/M AVAILABLE	WORD PROCESSING SOFTWARE AVAILABLE	ELECTRONIC SPREAD-SHEET	PROGRAMMING LANGUAGES INCLUDED	PROGRAMMING LANGUAGES AVAILABLE FROM MANUFACTURER	SOFTWARE AVAILABILITY	SERVICE AND SUPPORT	NOTES
TIMEX/ SINCLAIR 2068	Available from outside sources	No	Not too much	Included in ROM	No	N/A	N/A	Extended BASIC in ROM	None	Some through Sinclair and elsewhere	Through Sinclair, by mail	The newest product from Timex/Sinclair.
ATARI 800XL	Yes	Yes	Excellent through Atari and elsewhere	Included in ROM	Yes	Yes	Yes	Atari BASIC in ROM	Microsoft BASIC, Assembler, Pilot, LOGO	Good through Atari, excellent elsewhere	Good through Dealers and Authorized Service Centers	Very popular, well supported model.
COMMO-DORE 64	Yes	No	Good through Commodore	Included in ROM	Only with optional Z-80 CPU	Yes	No	BASIC, Assembler	None	Growing; a great deal is expected	Good through Dealers	Very popular system with the promise of full expansion.
ATARI 1200XL	Yes	Yes	Good through Atari and elsewhere	Included in ROM	No	Yes	Yes	Atari BASIC in ROM	Assembler, Microsoft BASIC, FORTH, LOGO, Pilot	Good through Atari; very good elsewhere	Good through Dealers and Authorized Service Centers	Upward compatible step for Atari 800XL users.

HARDWARE →

SYSTEM FEATURES	BASE PRICE	CPU TYPE	MEMORY (BYTES) RAM Standard Maximum	MEMORY (BYTES) ROM Standard Maximum	STORAGE	PRINTER (Unit or Interface)	DISPLAY SIZE (DIAGONAL) Lines x Chars	COLOR OR MONO-CHROME	KEYBOARD LAYOUT U/L CASE	GRAPHICS TYPE RESOLUTION	RS232 INTERFACE	SOUND CAPABILITY STANDARD
COLECO ADAM	under $1,000	Z-80A 8-bit	80K 144K (16K used for display)	N/A	Includes 500K (DataPack) high-speed Cassette Accepts ROM Cartridges	Included, letter-quality	Not Included Depends on Display 24 X 36	Color or Mono-chrome	Standard Both	Sprite Matrix and Symbols 256 x 192	Optional	Yes
RADIO SHACK TRS-80 MODEL 100 PORTABLE	under $1,000	8085 8-bit	8K 32K	32K 32K	Includes Cassette Interface	Interface Included	Included LCD type 8 X 40	Mono-chrome	Standard Both	Matrix 64 x 240	300 bps Modem Included	Yes
APPLE IIe	under $1,500	6502A 8-bit	64K 128K	6K 16K	Includes Cassette Interface Optional Floppy Disks	Interface Optional	Not Included Depends on Display 24 X 40 (80 cols. opt.)	Color or Mono-chrome	Standard Both	Matrix 280 x 192 B/W; 140 x 192 4 Colors	Optional	Yes
FRANKLIN ACE 1200	under $1,500	6502 & Z-80B Both 8-bit	64K for each CPU	N/A	Optional Floppy Disks	Interface Optional	Not Included Depends on Display 24 X 40 (80 cols.opt.)	Color or Mono-chrome	Standard Both	Matrix 280 x 192	Optional	Yes

	HARDWARE (cont.)			*SOFTWARE* →				PROGRAMMING LANGUAGES				
SYSTEM FEATURES	GAME PLAYING DEVICES AVAILABLE	SPEECH DEVICES AVAILABLE	HARDWARE EXPANSION	OPERATING SYSTEM	STANDARD CP/M AVAILABLE	WORD PROCESSING SOFTWARE AVAILABLE	ELECTRONIC SPREAD-SHEET	INCLUDED	AVAILABLE FROM MANUFACTURER	SOFTWARE AVAILABILITY	SERVICE AND SUPPORT	NOTES
COLECO ADAM	Yes (Coleco-Vision compatible)	No	Not much yet, but has 4 expansion slots	CP/M in ROM	Yes	Included in ROM	No	BASIC	LOGO	Good through CP/M sources when available in DataPacks	New system; support unknown	A great deal for the money. Should be very popular.
RADIO SHACK TRS-80 MODEL 100 PORTABLE	No	No	Limited from Radio Shack	Included in ROM	No	Included	No	BASIC in ROM	None	Scheduler, address book, WP, and communications included in ROM	Excellent from Radio Shack	An excellent portable workstation. Battery backup to 30 days.
APPLE IIe	Yes	Yes	Good through Apple, very good elsewhere	Included in ROM and on Disk	Yes, but requires outside vendor hardware	Yes	Yes	Extended BASIC in ROM	Pascal, Pilot, FORTRAN, LOGO, Assembler	Good through Apple, very good elsewhere	Good through Dealers	Very popular, well supported model.
FRANKLIN ACE 1200	Yes	Yes	Good through Franklin	Included in ROM	Yes	Included	Included	BASIC	C, COBOL, FORTH, FORTRAN, LOGO, Pascal	Good through dealers and Apple sources	Good through Dealers	An Apple look-alike that also runs Z-80 software.

HARDWARE →

SYSTEM FEATURES	BASE PRICE	CPU TYPE	MEMORY (BYTES) RAM Standard Maximum	ROM Standard Maximum	STORAGE	PRINTER (Unit or Interface)	DISPLAY SIZE (DIAGONAL) Lines x Chars	COLOR OR MONO-CHROME	KEYBOARD LAYOUT U/L CASE	GRAPHICS TYPE RESOLUTION	RS232 INTERFACE	SOUND CAPABILITY STANDARD
IBM PC JUNIOR (Enhanced Version)	under $1,500	8088 16-bit	128K 128K	64K 64K	Includes Cassette Interface 5¼'' Floppy Disk Included (360K) Accepts ROM Cartridges	Serial Printer Port Included	Not Included Depends on Display 24 X 80	Color or Mono-chrome	Standard Both	N/A	Optional	Yes
OSBORNE I	under $1,500	Z-80A 8-bit	64K 64K	4K 4K	Dual 5¼'' Floppy Disks Included (204K each)	Interface Included	Included 5'' 24 x 52 (24 x 80 optional)	Mono-chrome	Standard Both	Symbols	Included	No
IBM PERSONAL COMPUTER	under $2,000	8088 16-bit	64K 640K	40K 40K	Includes Cassette Interface Optional Floppy and Hard Disks	Interface Optional	Not Included Depends on Display 25 X 80	Color or Mono-chrome	Standard Both	Matrix and Symbols 640 x 200 B/W; 320 x 200 Color	Optional	Yes
KAYPRO II	under $2,000	Z-80 8-bit	64K 64K	2K 2K	Dual 5¼'' Floppy Disks Included (190K each)	Interface Included	Included 9'' 24 x 80	Mono-chrome	Standard Both	None	Included	No

	HARDWARE (cont.)			SOFTWARE →								
SYSTEM FEATURES	GAME PLAYING DEVICES AVAILABLE	SPEECH DEVICES AVAILABLE	HARDWARE EXPANSION	OPERATING SYSTEM	STANDARD CP/M AVAILABLE	WORD PROCESSING SOFTWARE AVAILABLE	ELECTRONIC SPREAD-SHEET	PROGRAMMING LANGUAGES INCLUDED	PROGRAMMING LANGUAGES AVAILABLE FROM MANUFACTURER	SOFTWARE AVAILABILITY	SERVICE AND SUPPORT	NOTES
IBM PC JUNIOR (Enhanced Version)	Yes	No	New system	PC-DOS in ROM	No	Yes	Yes	BASIC in ROM	LOGO	Good from IBM; excellent where compatible with PC software	New system; should be good	IBM's new entry into the home market. Due Feb. 1984.
OSBORNE I	No	No	Not much	CP/M on Disk	Yes	Included	Included	Extended BASIC, C-BASIC, Assembler	Pascal, FORTRAN	Software included; very good through CP/M sources	Uncertain following Osborne's bankruptcy	A well-established name with a very uncertain future.
IBM PERSONAL COMPUTER	Yes	No	Extremely good	PC-DOS in ROM and on Disk	16 bit	Yes	Yes	Extended BASIC in ROM and on Disk	Assembler, C-BASIC, Pascal, FORTRAN, COBOL	Excellent through outside sources, some from IBM	Good through Dealers	Very popular, well supported model.
KAYPRO II	No	No	Limited	CP/M on Disk	Yes	Included	Included	S-BASIC, M-BASIC	Assembler, C, COBOL, FORTH, FORTRAN, LISP, Pascal	Excellent software included; more through CP/M sources	Good through Dealers	A great deal for the money. Portable and popular.

HARDWARE →

SYSTEM FEATURES	BASE PRICE	CPU TYPE	MEMORY (BYTES) RAM Standard Maximum	MEMORY (BYTES) ROM Standard Maximum	STORAGE	PRINTER (Unit or Interface)	DISPLAY SIZE (DIAGONAL) Lines x Chars	COLOR OR MONO-CHROME	KEYBOARD LAYOUT U/L CASE	GRAPHICS TYPE RESOLUTION	RS232 INTERFACE	SOUND CAPABILITY STANDARD
MORROW MICRO DESIGN 3	under $2,000	Z-80A 8-bit	64K 128K	8K 8K	Includes Cassette Interface 5¼'' Floppy Disk Included (384K)	Interface Included	Included 12'' 24 x 80	Mono-chrome	Standard Both	Matrix and Symbols 720 x 288	Included	No
RADIO SHACK TRS-80 MODEL 4	under $2,000	Z-80A 8-bit	16K 128K	14K 14K	Includes Cassette Interface Dual 5¼'' Floppy Disks Included (184K each) Optional Hard	Interface Included	Included 12'' 24 x 80	Mono-chrome	Standard Both	Matrix and Symbols 640 x 240	Optional	Yes
TEXAS INSTRU-MENTS PROFES-SIONAL	under $2,000	8088 16-bit	64K 256K	8K 16K	Optional Floppy Disks	N/A	Not Included Depends on Display 25 X 80	Color or Mono-chrome	Standard Both	Matrix 720 x 300 8 Colors	Optional	Yes
HEATH H100/ ZENITH Z100	under $2,500 (kit) or $4,000 (assem-bled)	8088 16-bit 8085 8-bit	128K 768K	8K 32K	Includes Cassette Interface 5¼'' Floppy Disk Included (320K) Others Optional	Interface Included	Included 12'' 25 x 80	Color or Mono-chrome	Standard Both	Matrix 640 x 225	3 Included	No

	HARDWARE (cont.)			SOFTWARE →				PROGRAMMING LANGUAGES				
SYSTEM FEATURES	GAME PLAYING DEVICES AVAILABLE	SPEECH DEVICES AVAILABLE	HARDWARE EXPANSION	OPERATING SYSTEM	STANDARD CP/M AVAILABLE	WORD PROCESSING SOFTWARE AVAILABLE	ELECTRONIC SPREAD-SHEET	INCLUDED	AVAILABLE FROM MANUFACTURER	SOFTWARE AVAILABILITY	SERVICE AND SUPPORT	NOTES
MORROW MICRO DESIGN 3	No	No	Some from Morrow	CP/M on Disk	Yes	Included	Included	BASIC	Pilot	Good through CP/M sources; data base software included	Good through Dealers	Very good deal for the money.
RADIO SHACK TRS-80 MODEL 4	No	No	Good through Radio Shack, very good elsewhere	Included in ROM	Yes, but requires outside vendor hardware	Yes	Yes	Extended BASIC in ROM	C-BASIC, COBOL, FORTRAN, Assembler, LOGO, Pascal, Pilot	Good through Radio Shack, excellent elsewhere	Good through Dealers and Computer Centers	Very popular. Can use Model III software.
TEXAS INSTRU-MENTS PROFES-SIONAL	No	Yes	Good from TI and other sources	MS-DOS on Disk	16-bit	Yes	Yes	M-BASIC	Assembler, C-BASIC, C, COBOL, FORTRAN, Pascal	Excellent from TI and MS-DOS sources	Good through TI and Dealers	An excellent alternative to the IBM PC.
HEATH H100/ ZENITH Z100	Yes	Yes	Good through Heath/Zenith, Industry-Standard S-100 Bus	Several on Disk	Yes	Yes	Yes	None	BASIC, Compiler BASIC, Pascal, FORTRAN, COBOL, Assembler	Very good if using CP/M or MS-DOS	Good through Zenith/Heath Dealers. Some on-site servicing.	Kit or assembled. Very flexible system.

HARDWARE →

SYSTEM FEATURES	BASE PRICE	CPU TYPE	MEMORY (BYTES) RAM Standard Maximum	ROM Standard Maximum	STORAGE	PRINTER (Unit or Interface)	DISPLAY SIZE (DIAGONAL) Lines x Chars	COLOR OR MONO-CHROME	KEYBOARD LAYOUT U/L CASE	GRAPHICS TYPE RESOLUTION	RS232 INTERFACE	SOUND CAPABILITY STANDARD
APPLE III	under $3,000	6502A 8-bit	256K 256K	4K 4K	5¼'' Floppy Disk Included (143K) Others Optional	Interface Optional	Not Included Depends on Display 24 X 80 B/W 24 x 40 Color	Color or Mono-chrome	Standard Both	Matrix 560 x 192 B/W; 280 x 192 Color	Included	Yes
COMPAQ PORTABLE	under $3,000	8088 16-bit	128K 640K	N/A	Dual 5¼'' Floppy Disks Included (320K each)	Interface Included	Included 9'' 25 x 80	Color or Mono-chrome	Standard Both	Matrix 640 x 200	Included	No
DIGITAL EQUIPMENT CORP. RAIN-BOW 100	under $4,000	Z-80 8-bit 8088 16-bit	64K 256K	None	Dual 5¼'' Floppy Disks Included (400K each)	RS-232 Interface Included	Included 12'' 24 x 80 or 24 x 132	Mono-chrome (Color Optional)	Standard Both	Optional Matrix 800 x 240	Included	No
HEWLETT PACKARD HP-150	under $4,000	8088 16-bit	256K 640K	160K 160K	Dual 3½'' Disks Included (256K each)	Interface Included	Included (with touch sensors) 9'' 27 x 80	Mono-chrome	Standard Both	Matrix 512 x 390	2 Included	Yes

SYSTEM FEATURES	HARDWARE (cont.) GAME PLAYING DEVICES AVAILABLE	SPEECH DEVICES AVAILABLE	HARDWARE EXPANSION	SOFTWARE → OPERATING SYSTEM	STANDARD CP/M AVAILABLE	WORD PROCESSING SOFTWARE AVAILABLE	ELECTRONIC SPREAD-SHEET	PROGRAMMING LANGUAGES INCLUDED	PROGRAMMING LANGUAGES AVAILABLE FROM MANUFACTURER	SOFTWARE AVAILABILITY	SERVICE AND SUPPORT	NOTES
APPLE III	Yes	Yes	Good through Apple; not too much elsewhere	Included on Disk	Yes	Yes	Yes	None	Extended BASIC, COBOL, Pascal, Assembler	Very good when used in Apple II mode; not as much otherwise	Good through Dealers	A powerful system growing in popularity.
COMPAQ PORTABLE	No	No	Limited from Compaq	MS-DOS on Disk	16-bit	Yes	Yes	BASIC	COBOL, FORTRAN, Pascal	IBM PC-compatible; excellent from PC sources	Good through Dealers	Portable, rugged, and PC-compatible. An excellent value.
DIGITAL EQUIPMENT CORP. RAIN-BOW 100	No	No	Some from DEC	CP/M-86/80 on Disk	Yes	Yes	Yes	Assembler	BASIC, C, COBOL, FORTRAN, LISP, Pascal	Some from DEC; good through CP/M sources	Good from DEC	Has the largest manufacturer of mini-computers behind it.
HEWLETT PACKARD HP-150	No	No	New system; should be good from HP	MS-DOS on Disk	No	Yes	Yes	Microsoft BASIC	Pascal	Good through HP; excellent from MS-DOS sources	Good through HP and Dealers	A unique, touch-screen system that could become popular.

HARDWARE →

SYSTEM FEATURES	BASE PRICE	CPU TYPE	MEMORY (BYTES) RAM Standard Maximum	MEMORY (BYTES) ROM Standard Maximum	STORAGE	PRINTER (Unit or Interface)	DISPLAY SIZE (DIAGONAL) Lines x Chars	COLOR OR MONO-CHROME	KEYBOARD LAYOUT U/L CASE	GRAPHICS TYPE RESOLUTION	RS232 INTERFACE	SOUND CAPABILITY STANDARD
OTRONA ATTACHE	under $4,000	Z-80A 8-bit	64K 64K	None	Dual 5¼'' Floppy Disks Included (380K)	RS-232 Interface Included	Included 5½'' 24 x 80	Mono-chrome	Included Standard Both	Matrix 320 x 240	Included	Yes
RADIO SHACK TRS-80 MODEL 16	under $5,000	Z-80A 8-bit MC-68000 16-bit	256K 512K	None	8'' Floppy Disk Included (1250K) Others Optional	Interface Included	Included 12'' 24 x 80	Mono-chrome	Included Standard Both	Symbols	2 Included	No
VECTOR GRAPHIC VECTOR 4 VIP	under $5,000	Z-80B 8-bit 8088 16-bit	128K 256K	8K	Dual 5¼'' Floppy Disks Included (1200K)	Interface Included	Included 12'' 24 x 80	Mono-chrome	Included Standard Both	Matrix 640 x 312	Included	No
FORTUNE 32:16	under $5,000	MC-68000 16-bit	128K 1024K	4K 16K	5¼'' Floppy Disk Included (200K)	RS-232 Interface Included	Included 12'' 25 x 80	Mono-chrome	Included Standard Both	Optional Matrix 640 x 480	Included	No

HARDWARE (cont.) | *SOFTWARE* →

SYSTEM FEATURES	GAME PLAYING DEVICES AVAILABLE	SPEECH DEVICES AVAILABLE	HARDWARE EXPANSION	OPERATING SYSTEM	STANDARD CP/M AVAILABLE	WORD PROCESSING SOFTWARE AVAILABLE	ELECTRONIC SPREAD-SHEET	PROGRAMMING LANGUAGES INCLUDED	PROGRAMMING LANGUAGES AVAILABLE FROM MANUFACTURER	SOFTWARE AVAILABILITY	SERVICE AND SUPPORT	NOTES
OTRONA ATTACHE	No	No	Some from manufacturer; not too much elsewhere	CP/M included on Disk	Yes	Yes	Yes	BASIC Assembler	Pascal COBOL	Some from manufacturer; CP/M support still unknown	New system; support is unknown	A very portable, professional computer.
RADIO SHACK TRS-80 MODEL 16	No	No	Good through Radio Shack; not too much elsewhere	Two included on Disk	Yes	Yes	Yes	Assembler	Extended BASIC Compiler BASIC COBOL FORTRAN	Good through Radio Shack; also will accept CP/M	Good through Dealers and computer centers	Provides many business capabilities, & has many service & support locations.
VECTOR GRAPHIC VECTOR 4 VIP	No	No	Good through V.G. and elsewhere	CP/M and CP/M 86 included on Disk. MS-DOS available.	Yes	Yes Included	Yes Included	BASIC	COBOL Assembler FORTRAN Pascal	Good through V.G. and elsewhere	Through V.G. dealers and TRW	A new, capable, and expandable system.
FORTUNE 32:16	No	No	Some from Manufacturer; not too much elsewhere	Unix-like O.S. included on Disk	No	Yes	Yes	None	BASIC COBOL FORTRAN C Pascal	Some from manufacturer; not too much elsewhere	New system; support is unknown	A beautifully designed, professional system.

HARDWARE →

SYSTEM FEATURES	BASE PRICE	CPU TYPE	MEMORY (BYTES) RAM Standard Maximum	MEMORY (BYTES) ROM Standard Maximum	STORAGE	PRINTER (Unit or Interface)	DISPLAY SIZE (DIAGONAL) Lines x Chars	COLOR OR MONO-CHROME	KEYBOARD LAYOUT U/L CASE	GRAPHICS TYPE RESOLUTION	RS232 INTERFACE	SOUND CAPABILITY STANDARD
NORTH STAR ADVANTAGE 8/16	under $5,000	Z-80A 8-bit 8088 16-bit	64K 256K (+64K for Z-80A)	2K	Dual 5¼'' Floppy Disks Included (720K)	Interface Included	Included 12'' 24 x 80	Mono-chrome	Included Standard Both	Matrix 240 x 640	Included	No
VICTOR 9000	under $5,000	8088 16-bit	128K 896K	None	Dual 5¼'' Floppy Disks Included (1200K)	Interface Included	Included 12'' 25 x 80 or 50 x 132	Mono-chrome	Included Standard Both	Matrix 800 x 400	2 Included	No

SYSTEM FEATURES	GAME PLAYING DEVICES AVAILABLE	SPEECH DEVICES AVAILABLE	HARDWARE EXPANSION	OPERATING SYSTEM	STANDARD CP/M AVAILABLE	WORD PROCESSING SOFTWARE AVAILABLE	ELECTRONIC SPREAD-SHEET	PROGRAMMING LANGUAGES INCLUDED	PROGRAMMING LANGUAGES AVAILABLE FROM MANUFACTURER	SOFTWARE AVAILABILITY	SERVICE AND SUPPORT	NOTES
NORTH STAR ADVANTAGE 8/16	No	No	New system—not too much yet	CP/M, MS-DOS Optional	Yes	Yes	Yes	None	Extended BASIC, Compiler BASIC, Pascal, FORTRAN, C, COBOL	Very good if using CP/M; good through North Star	Good through dealers	An integrated, fast desktop model with excellent graphics capabilities.
VICTOR 9000	No	No	Some from manufacturer; not too much elsewhere	CP/M included on Disk	Yes	Yes	Yes	Assembler	Compiler BASIC COBOL	Some from manufacturer; CP/M support still unknown	New system; support is unknown	A well-designed business system.

HARDWARE (cont.) | SOFTWARE →